pwc

普华永道

普华永道国际财务报告准则实务指引系列（第十一册）
PricewaterhouseCoopers IFRS MOA Series (Volume Eleven)

Manual of Accounting — IFRS 2013

Chapter 7 - Foreign currencies

国际财务报告准则实务指引

第七章——外　币

中英文对照

翻译组主要成员：陈保郎　杨舒君　邱一林

U0823498

中国财政经济出版社

This book has been prepared for general guidance on matters of interest only, and does not constitute professional advice. You should not act upon the information contained in this book without obtaining specific professional advice. No representation or warranty (express or implied) is given as to the accuracy or completeness of the information contained in this book, and, to the extent permitted by law, PricewaterhouseCoopers does not accept or assume any liability, responsibility or duty of care for any consequences of you or anyone else acting, or refraining to act, in reliance on the information contained in this book or for any decision based on it.

This book covers one of the chapters of the English version and its Chinese translation, which the English version remains the definitive source of guidance. The publishers and the authors cannot accept any responsibility for any errors or misunderstandings arising from the English version and its Chinese translation. Neither can the publishers and the authors accept any responsibility for loss occasioned to any person acting or refraining from action as a result of the material in this book.

© 2013 PricewaterhouseCoopers. All rights reserved. "*PricewaterhouseCoopers*" and "*PwC*" refer to the network of member firms of PricewaterhouseCoopers International Limited ("*PwCIL*"). Each member firm is a separate legal entity and does not act as agent of PwCIL or any other member firm. PwCIL does not provide any services to clients. PwCIL is not responsible or liable for the acts or omissions of any of its member firms nor can it control the exercise of their professional judgment or bind them in any way. No member firm is responsible or liable for the acts or omissions of any other member firm nor can it control the exercise of another member firm's professional judgment or bind another member firm or PwCIL in any way.

编写本书之目的是对感兴趣的事项给予一般性的指导，而非提供专业建议。未征得具体专业意见之前，不应依据本书所述内容采取任何行动。我们不对书中所述信息是否准确或完整作出任何明示或暗示的承诺或保证。除非法律另有明文规定，普华永道不对任何个人或单位因为阅读了本书而采取或未采取某项行动的后果、或基于本书所作出的任何决定承担任何责任。

本书内容为英文本中的一个章节及其中文译文，指导概以英文为准。出版社和编译者不对英文原文及中文译文的偏差或误解承担任何责任，也不对任何个人或单位因为阅读了本书而采取或未采取某项行动所发生损失承担任何责任。

ⓒ 2013 普华永道（PricewaterhouseCoopers）版权所有。PricewaterhouseCoopers 及 PwC 泛指 PricewaterhouseCoopers International Limited（“*PwCIL*”）之成员机构网络。该机构网络中的每个成员均为独立的法律实体，不代表 PwCIL 或其他任何 PwCIL 的成员机构。PwCIL 不向客户提供任何服务。PwCIL 不为其成员机构的行为和疏忽担负责任，也不能影响成员机构的专业判断，对其不具有任何束缚。各成员机构不为其他成员机构的行为和疏忽担负责任，不影响他们的专业判断，对其他成员机构或 PwCIL 不具有任何束缚。

Preface

Recent years have seen major changes in financial reporting worldwide with the single most important change being convergence around IFRS. There has also been a keen focus to improve the long term development of the CPA profession within China. As the Ministry of Finance and other regulatory bodies continue to promulgate legislation to promote the development of the Chinese CPA profession, we hope the release of our IFRS Manual of Accounting with Chinese Translation will also contribute to this effort.

The Ministry of Finance issued the Accounting Standards for Business Enterprises (hereafter referred to as "China Accounting Standards" or "CAS") in 2006. CAS incorporates all of the principles of IFRS and there has been a continued focus on convergence over the last few years. Additionally, IFRS is becoming increasingly important for many companies in China, including domestic companies seeking to raise capital overseas, as well as for foreign companies that have operations in China. With the continued convergence of CAS and IFRS, the release of our IFRS Manual of Accounting with Chinese Translation brings to China the extensive collective experience of the PwC's global network of firms in applying IFRS.

We hope this Manual will play a part in promoting consistent, comparable, relevant and reliable IFRS financial information and will serve as a reference tool for accounting students, academics, practitioners and users of financial statements in better understanding and implementing IFRS. More importantly, we hope the advice given in this text will assist those dealing with the many issues faced in preparing IFRS financial statements and provide helpful insight to users of such statements.

Raymund Chao
Asia Pacific Assurance Leader
PwC

© 2013 PricewaterhouseCoopers LLP. All rights reserved.

前言

近年来，全球财务报告领域发生了重大变化，其中最为重要的一项变化是与国际财务报告准则的趋同。同时人们也热切地关注着中国境内注册会计师行业的长期发展。财政部及其他监管机构不断完善法规，推动中国注册会计师行业的发展，我们希望这本中英文对照的国际财务报告准则实务指引能够对此作出贡献。

财政部于2006年颁布了《企业会计准则》（以下称为中国会计准则，或CAS）。CAS包含了IFRS中的所有原则，且在过去的几年里持续趋同。此外，IFRS对于中国的许多公司来说越来越重要，包括寻求筹集海外资本的国内公司，以及在中国境内运营的外国公司。随着CAS与IFRS的持续趋同，本书的发行将给中国读者带来普华永道全球成员机构网络在应用IFRS方面积累的丰富的经验。

我们希望本书能够在推广一致的、可比的、相关的以及可靠的IFRS财务信息方面起到作用，并且可以作为会计领域的学生、学者、从业人员及财务报表使用者更好地理解及运用IFRS的参考工具。更为重要的是，我们希望本指引中提出的建议能够帮助其处理在编制IFRS财务报表时遇到的问题，并向此类财务报表使用者提供有用的观点。

赵柏基
普华永道亚太区审计部主管合伙人

ⓒ 2013 普华永道（PricewaterhouseCoopers）版权所有。

Overview/Introduction

The IFRS Manual of Accounting is a practical guide to International Financial Reporting Standards. With close to 70 countries that have converged their local accounting standards with IFRS as at the time of writing, the application of IFRS has attracted significant attention in the world stage. At the same time, as more and more countries adopt IFRS (or its equivalent local standard), views continue to develop or evolve as to how particular aspects of a standard should be interpreted and applied. The views expressed in this Manual are based on years of experience from PricewaterhouseCoopers' Global Accounting Consulting Services team. The views expressed are a guide to applying IFRS rather than a set of definitive interpretations. The application of IFRS to a specific company is a matter of judgement given its particular facts and circumstances. Moreover, the application of IFRS might be influenced by the views of regulators.

The Manual covers diverse areas of accounting from the recognition and measurement of financial instruments to accounting for deferred taxation, business combinations and share-based payments. It explains in detail the rules that apply to preparing consolidated financial statements and considers the other statements that appear in annual reports such as cash flow statements as well as disclosures required by each specific standard.

Due to the continued convergence of China Accounting Standards and IFRS, PwC China has undertaken a significant project to translate our Global IFRS Manual of Accounting into Chinese. We sincerely hope that our IFRS Manual of Accounting with Chinese Translation provides practical insights to transactions commonly-seen in China and can help preparers, auditors, analysts and other users of financial statements to bridge the gap between accounting principles and their applications.

Yvonne Kam
Accounting Consulting Service Lead Partner
PwC China and Hong Kong

© 2013 PricewaterhouseCoopers LLP. All rights reserved.

概述/引言

《国际财务报告准则实务指引》是应用国际财务报告准则的实务指南。于撰稿之时，已有近70个国家将其本国的会计准则与国际财务报告准则趋同，在世界范围内，国际财务报告准则的应用已广受重视。与此同时，随着越来越多的国家采用国际财务报告准则（或其等同的本地准则），关于某条准则特定方面应如何解释及应用的各种观点在持续发展或演变。本实务指引中所表达的观点是基于普华永道全球会计专业咨询服务团队以往多年的经验得出。我们所传达的观点是应用国际财务报告准则的指南，而非一系列确定的解释。一家特定的企业在应用国际财务报告准则时需根据特定的事实和环境作出判断。此外，国际财务报告准则的应用也可能受到监管机构观点的影响。

本实务指引涵盖从金融工具的确认和计量到递延税项、业务合并和以股份为基础的支付的核算等不同的会计领域。它详细解释了编制合并财务报表所应用的原则，并考虑了年报中出现的其他报表，如现金流量表以及每条特定准则所要求的披露。

鉴于中国会计准则与国际财务报告准则的持续趋同，普华永道中国启动了一项具有重大意义的项目，即将《国际财务报告准则实务指引》译成中文。我们诚挚地希望这套中英文对照的《国际财务报告准则实务指引》能够为中国常见的交易提供实用的见解，为编制者、审计人员、分析人员以及其他财务报表使用者们在会计原则与其具体应用之间架起一座桥梁。

金以文
会计专业咨询服务首席合伙人
普华永道中国及香港

ⓒ 2013 普华永道（PricewaterhouseCoopers）版权所有。

How to use this publication

Given the increasing importance of IFRS in China and the continued convergence of CAS and IFRS, the Accounting Consulting Services team of PwC China and Hong Kong have undertaken a significant project to translate the IFRS Manual of Accounting into Chinese.

The Manual is a practical guide in applying IFRS and the views are based on the extensive experience of the PwC's global network of firms. However, IFRS is not static and is continuously developing. The views on its interpretation and application will adapt and evolve. The views expressed in this Manual are a guide to applying IFRS rather than a set of definitive interpretations. The application of IFRS requires significant judgement and specific facts and circumstances should be carefully considered.

IFRS Manual of Accounting with Chinese Translation will be released in different volumes. Depending on the topic, each release may be a chapter or a combination of a number of chapters from the Manual.

Because of the interdependencies between individual IFRS, there are many cross references between different chapters of the Manual. Although the IFRS Manual of Accounting with Chinese Translation will be released in different volumes, the cross references have been maintained. Users are encouraged to refer to those cross references in other translated chapters or to the English version of the Manual if it helps in their understanding.

This book is the eleventh volume of IFRS Manual of Accounting Series with Chinese Translation. The content covers Chapter 7 – Foreign currencies of the English version and its translation. While every effort has been made to ensure an accurate translation, reference should be made to the English version in the event there are any differences between the Chinese and English versions.

© 2013 PricewaterhouseCoopers LLP. All rights reserved.

使用说明

鉴于 IFRS 在中国愈发重要以及 CAS 和 IFRS 的持续趋同，普华永道中国及香港的会计专业咨询服务小组已着手开始了一项具有重大意义的项目，即将《国际财务报告准则实务指引》译成中文。

《国际财务报告准则实务指引》是对应用 IFRS 的实务指引，其中的观点是基于普华永道全球成员机构网络丰富的经验。然而，IFRS 不是静止的，而是持续发展的；因此，对 IFRS 的解释和适用会有所改变和发展。本指引表达的观点是对应用 IFRS 的一种指引，而非一套具有决定性的解释。IFRS 的应用需要大量的判断，还应当谨慎考虑特定的事实及所处的环境。

IFRS 实务指引及其中文翻译版将分成多册发行。根据主题，每一册可能是本指引的某一章节或是包含某几个章节。

由于各个 IFRS 准则之间的相互依存，因此本指引中不同的章节会相互参照索引。尽管 IFRS 实务指引及其中文翻译版将分成多册发行，但仍保留此类相互参照索引。如果有助于理解，我们鼓励读者阅读此类相互参照索引时参考其他已翻译的章节或指引的英文版。

本书为普华永道国际财务报告准则实务指引系列（中英文对照）的第十一册。内容为英文原版的《国际财务报告准则实务指引》中的《第七章——外币》。我们已尽最大的努力来确保翻译的准确，但中文翻译版与英文版出现不一致时，应参考英文版。

ⓒ 2013 普华永道（PricewaterhouseCoopers）版权所有。

The chapters of our IFRS Manual of Accounting have been restructured in 2013 and changes have been marked as follow:

IFRS Manual of Accounting (MoA)

Accounting rules and principles

01 – Introduction

02 – Accounting principles and applicability of IFRS (combined with chapter 1 in MoA 2013)

03 – First-time adoption of IFRS

04 – Presentation of financial statements

05 – Accounting policies, accounting estimates and errors (chapter 3 in MoA 2013)

06 – Hyper-inflation (chapter 31 in MoA 2013)

07 – Foreign currencies

08 – Insurance contracts

Income statement and related notes

09 – Revenue and construction contracts

10 – Segment reporting

11 – Employee benefits

11A – Employee benefits (IAS 19 revised)

12 – Share-based payment

13 – Taxation

14 – Earnings per share

Balance sheet and related notes

15 – Intangible assets

16 – Property, plant and equipment

17 – Investment property

18 – Impairment of assets

19 – Lease accounting

20 – Inventories

© 2013 PricewaterhouseCoopers LLP. All rights reserved.

英文原版《国际财务报告准则实务指引》的章节已在 2013 年再版时重新排列，变动已列示如下：

国际财务报告准则实务指引

会计规则和原则

01 – 引言
02 – 会计原则和国际财务报告准则的适用性（在 2013 版中与第一章合并）

03 – 首次采用国际财务报告准则
04 – 财务报表的列报
05 – 会计政策、会计估计和差错（在 2013 版中为第三章）
06 – 恶性通货膨胀（在 2013 版中为第三十一章）
07 – 外币
08 – 保险合同

利润表及相关附注

09 – 收入与建造合同
10 – 分部报告
11 – 职工福利
11A – 职工福利（IAS 19 修订版）
12 – 以股份为基础的支付（“股份支付”）
13 – 所得税会计
14 – 每股收益

资产负债表及相关附注

15 – 无形资产
16 – 不动产、工厂和设备
17 – 投资性房地产
18 – 资产减值
19 – 租赁会计
20 – 存货

© 2013 普华永道（PricewaterhouseCoopers）版权所有。

21 – Provisions and contingencies
22 – Events after the reporting period and financial commitments
23 – Share capital and reserves

Consolidated financial statements

24 – Consolidated and separate financial statements
24A – Consolidated financial statements
25 – Business combinations
26 – Disposal of subsidiaries, businesses and non-current assets
27 – Equity accounting
28 – Joint ventures
28A – Joint arrangements

Other subjects

29 – Related party disclosures
30 – Cash flow statements
31 – Interim reports and preliminary announcements (seperate book in 2013)
32 – Agriculture
33 – Service concession arrangements
34 – Fair Value (chapter 5 in MoA 2013)
35 – Management commentery

IFRS Manual of Accounting—Financial Instruments (chapter 6 in MoA 2013)

01 – Overview (chapter 6. 1 in MoA 2013)
02 – Introduction (combined with chapter 6. 1 in MoA 2013)
03 – Objectives and scope of IAS 32, IAS 39 and IFRS 7 (combined with chapter 6. 1 in MoA 2013)
04 – Nature and characteristics of financial instruments (chapter 6. 2 in MoA 2013)
05 – Embedded derivatives in host contracts (chapter 6. 3 in MoA 2013)

© 2013 PricewaterhouseCoopers LLP. All rights reserved.

21 – 准备和或有事项
22 – 报告期后事项和财务承诺
23 – 股本和准备金

合并财务报表
24 – 合并财务报表和单独财务报表
24A – 合并财务报表
25 – 业务合并
26 – 子公司、业务和非流动资产的处置
27 – 权益法核算
28 – 合营
28A – 合营安排

其他主题
29 – 关联方披露
30 – 现金流量表
31 – 中期报告和初步公告（在2013版中单独成书）
32 – 农业
33 – 服务特许权安排
34 – 公允价值（在2013版中为第五章）
35 – 管理层评注

国际财务报告准则实务指引——金融工具（在2013版中为第六章）

01 – 概览（在2013版中为第6.1章）
02 – 引言（在2013版中与第6.1章合并）
03 – 国际会计准则第32号、国际会计准则第39号及国际财务报告准则第7号的目标与范围（在2013版中与第6.1章合并）
04 – 金融工具的性质和特征（在2013版中为第6.2章）

05 – 主合同中的嵌入衍生工具（在2013版中为第6.3章）

ⓒ 2013 普华永道（PricewaterhouseCoopers）版权所有。

06 – Classification of financial instruments (chapter 6. 4 in MoA 2013)
07 – Financial liabilities and equity (chapter 6. 5 in MoA 2013)
08 – Recognition and derecognition (chapter 6. 6 in MoA 2013)
09 – Measurement of financial assets and liabilities (chapter 6. 7 in MoA 2013)
10 – Hedge accounting (chapter 6. 8 in MoA 2013)
11 – Presentation and disclosure (chapter 6. 9 in MoA 2013)
12 – IFRS 9, "Financial Instruments" (chapter 6. 10 in MoA 2013)

© 2013 PricewaterhouseCoopers LLP. All rights reserved.

06 – 金融工具的分类（在 2013 版中为第 6. 4 章）

07 – 金融负债和权益（在 2013 版中为第 6. 5 章）

08 – 确认和终止确认（在 2013 版中为第 6. 6 章）

09 – 金融资产和金融负债的计量（在 2013 版中为第 6. 7 章）

10 – 套期会计（在 2013 版中为第 6. 8 章）

11 – 列报和披露（在 2013 版中为第 6. 9 章）

12 – 国际财务报告准则第 9 号——金融工具（在 2013 版中为第 6. 10 章）

ⓒ 2013 普华永道（PricewaterhouseCoopers）版权所有。

International standards and interpretations

International standards

IFRS 1	First-time adoption of International Financial Reporting Standards
IFRS 2	Share-based payment
IFRS 3	Business combinations
IFRS 4	Insurance contracts
IFRS 5	Non-current assets held for sale and discontinued operations
IFRS 6	Exploration for and evaluation of mineral resources
IFRS 7	Financial instruments: Disclosures
IFRS 8	Operating segments
IFRS 9	Financial instruments
IFRS 10	Consolidated financial statements
IFRS 11	Joint arrangements
IFRS 12	Disclosure of interests in other entities
IFRS 13	Fair value measurement
IAS 1	Presentation of financial statements
IAS 2	Inventories
IAS 7	Cash flow statements
IAS 8	Accounting policies, changes in accounting estimates and errors
IAS 10	Events after the balance sheet date
IAS 11	Construction contracts
IAS 12	Income taxes
IAS 16	Property, plant and equipment
IAS 17	Leases
IAS 18	Revenue
IAS 19	Employee benefits
IAS 20	Accounting for government grants and disclosure of government assistance
IAS 21	The effects of changes in foreign exchange rates
IAS 23	Borrowing costs

© 2013 PricewaterhouseCoopers LLP. All rights reserved.

国际财务报告准则及解释公告

国际财务报告准则

国际财务报告准则第 1 号	首次采用国际财务报告准则
国际财务报告准则第 2 号	以股份为基础的支付
国际财务报告准则第 3 号	企业合并
国际财务报告准则第 4 号	保险合同
国际财务报告准则第 5 号	持有待售的非流动资产和终止经营
国际财务报告准则第 6 号	矿产资源的勘探和评价
国际财务报告准则第 7 号	金融工具：披露
国际财务报告准则第 8 号	经营分部
国际财务报告准则第 9 号	金融工具
国际财务报告准则第 10 号	合并财务报表
国际财务报告准则第 11 号	合营安排
国际财务报告准则第 12 号	对其他主体中权益的披露
国际财务报告准则第 13 号	公允价值计量
国际会计准则第 1 号	财务报表的列报
国际会计准则第 2 号	存货
国际会计准则第 7 号	现金流量表
国际会计准则第 8 号	会计政策、会计估计变更和差错
国际会计准则第 10 号	报告期后事项
国际会计准则第 11 号	建造合同
国际会计准则第 12 号	所得税
国际会计准则第 16 号	不动产、工厂和设备
国际会计准则第 17 号	租赁
国际会计准则第 18 号	收入
国际会计准则第 19 号	职工福利
国际会计准则第 20 号	政府补助的会计和政府援助的披露
国际会计准则第 21 号	汇率变动的影响
国际会计准则第 23 号	借款费用

ⓒ 2013 普华永道（PricewaterhouseCoopers）版权所有。

IAS 24	Related-party disclosures
IAS 26	Accounting and reporting by retirement benefit plans
IAS 27	Consolidated and separate financial statements
IAS 28	Investments in associates
IAS 29	Financial reporting in hyper-inflationary economies
IAS 31	Interests in joint ventures
IAS 32	Financial instruments: Presentation
IAS 33	Earnings per share
IAS 34	Interim financial reporting
IAS 36	Impairment of assets
IAS 37	Provisions, contingent liabilities and contingent assets
IAS 38	Intangible assets
IAS 39	Financial instruments: Recognition and measurement
IAS 40	Investment property
IAS 41	Agriculture

Interpretations

IFRIC 1	Changes in existing decommissioning, restoration and similar liabilities
IFRIC 2	Members' shares in co-operative entities and similar Instruments
IFRIC 4	Determining whether an arrangement contains a lease
IFRIC 5	Rights to interests arising from decommissioning, restoration and environmental rehabilitation funds
IFRIC 6	Liabilities arising from participating in a specific market - Waste electrical and electronic equipment
IFRIC 7	Applying the restatement approach under IAS 29 Financial reporting in hyper-inflationary economies
IFRIC 8	Scope of IFRS 2
IFRIC 9	Re-assessment of embedded derivatives
IFRIC 10	Interim financial reporting and impairment
IFRIC 11	IFRS 2 - Group and treasury share transactions
IFRIC 12	Service concession arrangements

© 2013 PricewaterhouseCoopers LLP. All rights reserved.

国际会计准则第 24 号	关联方披露
国际会计准则第 26 号	退休福利计划的会计和报告
国际会计准则第 27 号	合并财务报表和单独财务报表
国际会计准则第 28 号	联营中的投资
国际会计准则第 29 号	恶性通货膨胀经济中的财务报告
国际会计准则第 31 号	合营中的权益
国际会计准则第 32 号	金融工具：列报
国际会计准则第 33 号	每股收益
国际会计准则第 34 号	中期财务报告
国际会计准则第 36 号	资产减值
国际会计准则第 37 号	准备、或有负债和或有资产
国际会计准则第 38 号	无形资产
国际会计准则第 39 号	金融工具：确认和计量
国际会计准则第 40 号	投资性房地产
国际会计准则第 41 号	农业

解释公告

国际财务报告解释公告第 1 号	现有退役、复原和类似负债的变动
国际财务报告解释公告第 2 号	成员在合作主体中的股份和类似工具
国际财务报告解释公告第 4 号	确定一项协议是否包含租赁
国际财务报告解释公告第 5 号	退役、复原和环境恢复基金产生的权益
国际财务报告解释公告第 6 号	参与废弃电器和电子设备特定市场产生的负债
国际财务报告解释公告第 7 号	应用《国际会计准则第 29 号——恶性通货膨胀经济中的财务报告》中的重述法
国际财务报告解释公告第 8 号	《国际财务报告准则第 2 号》的范围
国际财务报告解释公告第 9 号	嵌入衍生工具的重估
国际财务报告解释公告第 10 号	中期财务报告和减值
国际财务报告解释公告第 11 号	《国际财务报告准则第 2 号》：集团和库藏股交易
国际财务报告解释公告第 12 号	特许服务权安排

ⓒ 2013 普华永道（PricewaterhouseCoopers）版权所有。

IFRIC 13	Customer loyalty programmes
IFRIC 14	IAS 19 – The limit on a defined benefit asset, minimum funding requirements and their interaction
IFRIC 15	Agreements for the construction of real estate
IFRIC 16	Hedges of a net investment in a foreign operation
IFRIC 17	Distributions of non-cash assets to owners
IFRIC 18	Transfers of assets from customers
IFRIC 19	Extinguishing financial liabilities with equity instruments
IFRIC 20	Stripping costs in the production phase of a surface mine
SIC 7	Introduction of the euro
SIC 10	Government Assistance – No specific relation to operating activities
SIC 12	Consolidation – Special purpose entities
SIC 13	Jointly controlled entities – Non-Monetary contributions by venturers
SIC 15	Operating leases – Incentives
SIC 21	Income taxes – Recovery of revalued non-depreciable assets
SIC 25	Income taxes – Changes in the tax status of an entity or its shareholders
SIC 27	Evaluating the substance of transactions in the legal form of a lease
SIC 29	Service Concession Arrangements: Disclosures
SIC 31	Revenue – Barter transactions involving advertising services
SIC 32	Intangible assets – Web site costs

© 2013 PricewaterhouseCoopers LLP. All rights reserved.

国际财务报告解释公告第 13 号	客户忠诚度计划
国际财务报告解释公告第 14 号	《国际会计准则第 19 号》：对设定受益资产的限制、最低资金要求及其相互作用
国际财务报告解释公告第 15 号	房地产建造合同
国际财务报告解释公告第 16 号	对境外经营净投资的套期
国际财务报告解释公告第 17 号	以非现金资产对所有者进行分配
国际财务报告解释公告第 18 号	从客户处转移资产
国际财务报告解释公告第 19 号	以权益工具解除金融负债
国际财务报告解释公告第 20 号	露天矿生产阶段的剥离成本
国际会计准则解释公告第 7 号	引入欧元
国际会计准则解释公告第 10 号	政府援助：与经营活动没有特定联系的政府援助
国际会计准则解释公告第 12 号	合并：特殊目的主体
国际会计准则解释公告第 13 号	共同控制主体：合营者的非货币性投入
国际会计准则解释公告第 15 号	经营租赁：激励措施
国际会计准则解释公告第 21 号	所得税：已重估非折旧资产的收回
国际会计准则解释公告第 25 号	所得税：主体或其股东纳税状况的改变
国际会计准则解释公告第 27 号	评价涉及租赁法律形式的交易实质
国际会计准则解释公告第 29 号	特许服务权安排：披露
国际会计准则解释公告第 31 号	收入：涉及广告服务的易货交易
国际会计准则解释公告第 32 号	无形资产：网站成本

ⓒ 2013 普华永道（PricewaterhouseCoopers）版权所有。

Abbreviations and terms used

Accounts	financial statements
AG	Application Guidance
App	Appendix
ARC	Accounting Regulatory Committee
BC	Basis for Conclusions (to an accounting standard)
C	currency unit
Chp	Chapter
chapter (1)	'PricewaterhouseCoopers' Manual of accounting' – chapter (1)
CESR	Committee of European Securities Regulators
CPP	current purchasing power
DP	discussion paper
EBIT	earnings before interest and tax
EBITDA	earnings before interest, tax, depreciation and amortisation
ED	exposure draft
EFRAG	European Financial Reporting Advisory Group
EPS	earnings per share
EU	European Union
FASB	Financial Accounting Standards Board (US)
Framework	Framework for the preparation and presentation of financial statements
GAAP	generally accepted accounting principles (and practices)
IAS	International Accounting Standard (see also IFRS)
IASB	International Accounting Standards Board
IFRIC	International Financial Reporting Interpretations Committee
IFRS	International Financial Reporting Standard (see also IAS)
IG	Implementation Guidance (to an accounting standard)

© 2013 PricewaterhouseCoopers LLP. All rights reserved.

缩写及词汇对照

财务报表
实施指南
附录
会计监管委员会
（某一准则的）结论基础
货币单位
章
第一章（普华永道《国际财务报告准则实务指引》——第一章）

欧洲证券监管委员会
现行购买力
讨论稿
息税前收益
扣除利息、所得税、折旧和摊销之前的收益
征求意见稿
欧洲财务报告咨询组
每股收益
欧盟
（美国）财务会计准则委员会
编报财务报表的框架

公认会计原则
国际会计准则（亦请参见 IFRS）
国际会计准则理事会
国际财务报告解释委员会
国际财务报告准则（亦请参见 IAS）
（某一准则的）应用指南

© 2013 普华永道（PricewaterhouseCoopers）版权所有。

para(s)	paragraph(s) of Schedules to the Companies Acts, or IFRSs or IASs or FRSs, or SSAPs, or FREDs, or EDs, or DPs, or text
PPE	property, plant and equipment
US SEC	US Securities and Exchange Commission
SIC	Standing Interpretation Committee of the IASC (see IFRIC)
SPE	special purpose entity
UK	United Kingdom
US	United States of America

© 2013 PricewaterhouseCoopers LLP. All rights reserved.

段落（公司法、国际财务报告准则、国际会计准则、财务报告准则、会计实务准则、财务报告征求意见稿、征求意见稿、讨论稿或文章中的段落）

不动产、工厂和设备
美国证券交易委员会
国际会计准则委员会的常设解释委员会（参见 IFRIC）

特殊目的主体
英国
美国

ⓒ 2013 普华永道（PricewaterhouseCoopers）版权所有。

Chapter 7 Foreign currencies

Contents

© 2013 PricewaterhouseCoopers LLP. All rights reserved.

第七章　外　　币

目　录

ⓒ 2013 普华永道（PricewaterhouseCoopers）版权所有。

© 2013 PricewaterhouseCoopers LLP. All rights reserved.

ⓒ 2013 普华永道（PricewaterhouseCoopers）版权所有。

Introduction

7.1 Entities conduct businesses that are not confined within national boundaries. The globalisation of markets for goods and services as well as capital means entities have to engage in international trade, cross-border alliances and joint ventures if they are to survive and grow in today's competitive business environment. Entities conduct business in the international market place in a number of ways. First, entities may buy goods and services from overseas suppliers and sell goods and services to overseas customers. Secondly, they may extend their international reach by conducting business through overseas subsidiaries, branches and associates.

7.2 In the first situation, transactions are often expressed in foreign currencies. The results of these transactions are translated into the entity's functional currency for financial reporting purposes. In the second situation, it is usual for the foreign operation to maintain its accounting records in the currency of the primary economic environment in which it operates. It is not possible to combine, add or subtract measurements expressed in different currencies, so management translates the foreign operation's results and financial position into the currency in which the reporting entity presents its consolidated financial statements.

7.3 Accounting for foreign currencies is, therefore, primarily concerned with the translation process whereby financial data denominated in one currency is expressed in terms of another currency. The translation process does not change the essential characteristics of the assets and liabilities measured. It merely restates assets and liabilities, initially expressed in a foreign currency unit, to a common currency unit by applying a rate of exchange factor – a translation rate.

7.4 Different translation rates may be used depending on the circumstances. These are:

- The historical rate – the rate of exchange ruling at the date the transaction or revaluation occurred.
- The closing rate – the rate ruling at the balance sheet date.
- The average rate ruling during the year.

© 2013 PricewaterhouseCoopers LLP. All rights reserved.

引言

7.1　主体并不局限在其所在的国家境内开展业务，商品、服务及资本市场的全球化意味着主体如果要在当今竞争激烈的商业环境中谋求生存和发展，必须从事国际贸易、跨国联盟及合营。主体以多种方式在国际市场开展业务。首先，主体可能从海外供应商购买商品和服务，并向海外客户销售商品和服务；其次，主体可能通过其海外子公司、分公司及联营开展业务以扩展其在国际上的覆盖范围。

7.2　在第一种情形下，交易通常以外币表示，为了财务报告的需要，这些交易会折算为主体的功能货币。在第二种情形下，境外经营通常以其经营所处的主要经济环境中的货币进行会计记录。由于以不同币种表示的计量结果无法汇总或相加减，因此管理层将境外经营的成果和财务状况折算为报告主体列报其合并财务报表所使用的货币。

7.3　因此，外币的会计处理主要是涉及将以某一种货币计价的财务数据以另一种货币表示的折算过程。这一折算过程不会改变所计量的资产和负债的本质特征，而是仅仅将最初以某一外币表示的资产和负债通过一个换算率（即折算率）而转换为一个通用的货币单位重新列示。

7.4　根据不同情况可能使用不同的折算率，折算率有以下几种：

- 历史汇率——交易日或重估日的汇率。
- 期末汇率——资产负债表日的汇率。
- 年度平均汇率。

ⓒ 2013 普华永道（PricewaterhouseCoopers）版权所有。

The average rate is generally confined to income and expenditure items. The rates used for balance sheet items (historical or closing) depend on the types of assets and liabilities – monetary or non-monetary. These methods are addressed later in this chapter.

7.5 The treatment of exchange differences that arise on foreign currency transactions is different from those that arise on foreign currency translation. Foreign currency translation also raises a number of questions, such as: the extent to which exchange gains and losses from different sources can be offset; whether some exchange differences should be recognised immediately whilst others should be deferred; and whether the recognition should be through the income statement or in other comprehensive income.

[The next paragraph is 7.23.]

Objectives

7.23 IAS 21 prescribes how to:

- Include foreign currency transactions and foreign operations in an entity's financial statements.
- Specify which exchange rates to use and how to report the effects of changes in exchange rates in the financial statements.
- Translate the financial statements into a presentation currency.

[IAS 21 paras 1, 2].

Applying these requirements in practice can be complex. This chapter provides guidance on the issues commonly encountered.

Scope

7.24 IAS 21 sets out the requirements for foreign currency translation. It applies to any entity that comes within its scope and engages in foreign currency

© 2013 PricewaterhouseCoopers LLP. All rights reserved.

平均汇率一般仅限于损益项目；用于资产负债表项目的汇率（历史汇率或期末汇率）取决于资产和负债的类型，即货币性项目或非货币性项目。本章的下文将对这些方法进行阐述。

7.5　由外币交易产生的汇兑差额的处理不同于由外币折算产生的汇兑差额的处理。外币折算也引发了多个问题，例如：由不同来源产生的汇兑损益可否相互抵销；某些汇兑差额是否应于当期确认，而其他部分是否应予以递延；以及汇兑损益应通过利润表还是其他综合收益予以确认。

[下一段为第 7.23 段。]

目标

7.23　IAS 21 旨在规范：

- 如何将外币交易和境外经营包含在主体的财务报表中。
- 如何明确使用哪一种汇率以及如何在财务报表中报告汇率变动的影响。
- 如何将财务报表折算成列报货币。

[IAS 21 第 1、2 段]。

在实务中应用这些要求可能是复杂的。本章将对那些普遍遇到的问题提供指引。

适用范围

7.24　IAS 21 列出了外币折算的要求，适用于任何在其范围内并且从事涉及外币的经营活动的主体。该准则适用于：

© 2013 普华永道（PricewaterhouseCoopers）版权所有。

operations. The standard is applied in:

- Accounting for transactions and balances in foreign currencies, except for those derivative transactions and balances that are within the scope of IAS 39.
- Translating the results and financial position of foreign operations that are included in the entity's financial statements by consolidation, proportionate consolidation or equity accounting.
- Translating an entity's results and financial position into a presentation currency.

[IAS 21 para 3].

7.25 Accounting for foreign currency derivatives is scoped out of IAS 21 (and included in IAS 39). Foreign currency derivatives that may be embedded in various contracts and that require separate accounting under IAS 39 are scoped out of IAS 21; embedded foreign currency derivatives that do not require separate accounting under IAS 39 are included in IAS 21. However, IAS 21 applies to translation of foreign currency derivatives from a functional currency to a presentation currency. [IAS 21 para 4].

7.26 The standard does not apply to hedge accounting for foreign currency items, including the hedging of a net investment in a foreign operation. These issues are addressed in IAS 39. [IAS 21 para 5]. See chapter 10 of IFRS Manual of Accounting – Financial Instruments.

The functional currency approach

Introduction

7.27 IAS 21 requires each individual entity to determine its functional currency and measure its results and financial position in that currency. Each individual entity included in the consolidation therefore has its own functional currency. There is no such thing as a group functional currency.

7.28 The requirement to identify each entity's functional currency is the key

© 2013 PricewaterhouseCoopers LLP. All rights reserved.

- 除在 IAS 39 范围内的衍生工具交易和余额以外的外币交易和余额的会计处理。
- 通过合并、比例合并或权益法被包含在主体财务报表中的境外经营的成果和财务状况的折算。
- 将主体的经营成果和财务状况折算为列报货币。

[IAS 21 第 3 段]。

7.25　外币衍生工具的会计处理被排除在 IAS 21 的范围之外（而是被包含在 IAS 39 中）。那些可能嵌入各种合同，并且根据 IAS 39 需要单独核算的外币衍生工具不在 IAS 21 的适用范围内；而那些根据 IAS 39 不需要单独核算的外币衍生工具，则包含在 IAS 21 的适用范围内。然而，IAS 21 适用于将外币衍生工具从功能货币折算为列报货币。[IAS 21 第 4 段]。

7.26　该准则不适用于外币项目的套期会计（包括对境外经营净投资的套期）。这些问题由 IAS 39 进行规范。[IAS 21 第 5 段]。参见《国际财务报告准则实务指引——金融工具系列》第十章。

功能货币法

引言

7.27　IAS 21 要求各个个别主体确定其功能货币，并以该功能货币计量其经营成果和财务状况。因此，包含在合并范围内的每一个别主体均有其各自的功能货币，并不存在所谓的集团功能货币。

7.28　IAS 21 的关键特点是要求识别每一主体的功能货币。功能货币是决定

© 2013 普华永道（PricewaterhouseCoopers）版权所有。

feature of IAS 21. The functional currency serves as the basis for determining whether the entity is engaging in foreign currency transactions. This is because IAS 21 defines foreign currency as a currency other than the functional currency. [IAS 21 para 8]. Additionally, identifying the functional currency has a direct impact on the treatment of exchange gains and losses arising from the translation process and, thereby, the reported results, as will be evident later. IAS 21 provides guidance on determining the functional currency, which is considered from paragraph 7.31 below.

Example – Identification of foreign currency transactions

An entity trades in crude oil and has a US dollar functional currency per the assessment required under IAS 21, because substantially all of its sales and purchases are in US dollars. The entity is located in London and has significant transactions in sterling. It has issued euro-denominated share capital to its Dutch parent. Transactions with the parent are denominated in euros.

The sterling transactions and euro transactions are foreign currency transactions because the entity has a US dollar functional currency. The entity's physical location and the denomination of its share capital do not change the treatment of sterling – and euro – denominated transactions.

[The next paragraph is 7.31.]

Determining the functional currency

7.31 An entity's functional currency is a matter of fact. In some cases, the facts will clearly identify the functional currency. In other cases they will not and judgement will be required. IAS 21 provides guidance on how to determine an entity's functional currency.

7.31.1 An entity's functional currency is the currency of the primary economic environment in which it operates. [IAS 21 para 8]. It should, therefore, be determined at the entity level. An entity includes a foreign operation, that is, a subsidiary, associate, branch or joint venture whose activities are based or conducted in a country or currency other than that of the reporting entity.

© 2013 PricewaterhouseCoopers LLP. All rights reserved.

主体是否从事外币交易的基础；这是因为 IAS 21 将外币定义为功能货币之外的货币。[IAS 21 第 8 段]。此外，识别功能货币直接影响折算过程中产生的汇兑损益的处理、进而影响报告的经营成果，这将在后文中可以明显看出来。IAS 21 提供了关于确定功能货币的指引，这在下文第 7. 31 段起进行讨论。

示例——外币交易的识别

某主体从事原油贸易，按照 IAS 21 的要求所进行的评价，美元为其功能货币，因为其实质上所有的销售和采购都是以美元计价的。该主体位于伦敦，有大量的以英镑进行的交易。其向荷兰母公司发行了以欧元计价的股本，与母公司之间的交易以欧元计价。

因为该主体的功能货币为美元，所以以英镑和欧元进行的交易属于外币交易。主体的地理位置和其股本的计价不改变以英镑和欧元计价的交易的处理。

[下一段为第 7. 31 段。]

功能货币的确定

7. 31　主体的功能货币是根据事实而定的。在某些情况下，事实将清晰地识别出功能货币；而在其他一些情况下则不然，将必须进行判断。IAS 21 就如何确定某一主体的功能货币提供了指引。

7. 31. 1　某一主体的功能货币是其经营所处的主要经济环境中的货币。[IAS 21 第 8 段]。因此，其应当在主体层面进行确定。这里所指的主体包含境外经营，即经营场所或经营活动在报告主体所在国以外的国家或采用报告主体所使用货币以外的货币的子公司、联营、分支机构或合营。

ⓒ 2013 普华永道（PricewaterhouseCoopers）版权所有。

7.31.2 An individual entity (including a foreign operation) for these purposes may not correspond to a legal entity (for example, a company). For example, a branch that is part of a single legal entity may be a foreign operation. Judgement is required in determining an entity's functional currency based on individual facts and circumstances.

7.31.3 A group comprised of multiple entities identifies the functional currency of each entity for the purpose of defining that entity's foreign currency exposure. Different entities within a multinational group, therefore, often have different functional currencies. The group as a whole does not have a functional currency.

7.32 The primary economic environment in which an entity operates is normally the economic environment in which it primarily generates and expends cash. [IAS 21 para 9]. The functional currency is normally the currency of the country in which the entity is located. It may, however, be a different currency. In addition, circumstances might indicate that the foreign operation's functional currency is the same as the reporting entity's functional currency. For this purpose, a foreign operation is defined as an entity that is a subsidiary, associate, joint venture or a branch of the reporting entity, the activities of which are based or conducted in a country or currency other than that of the reporting entity. [IAS 21 para 8].

7.33 IAS 21 requires entities to consider primary and secondary indicators when determining the functional currency. Primary indicators are closely linked to the primary economic environment in which the entity operates and are given more weight. Secondary indicators provide supporting evidence to determine an entity's functional currency. Both of these indicators and the factors needing consideration are shown in the table below.

Primary indicators of functional currency [IAS 21 para 9]	
Indicators	**Factors to be considered by the entity in determining the functional currency**
Sales and cash inflows	(a) The currency that *mainly influences* sales prices for its goods and services. This will often be the currency in which sales prices for goods and services are denominated and settled. [IAS 21 para 9(a)(i)]. In other words, where an active local sales market exists for the entity's products that are also priced in the local currency, and revenues are collected primarily in that local

© 2013 PricewaterhouseCoopers LLP. All rights reserved.

7.31.2 就确定功能货币而言，一个个别主体（包括一个境外经营）可能并不等同于一个法人主体（如一家公司）。例如，作为单个法人主体的一部分的一个分支机构可能是一个境外经营。确定某一主体的功能货币需要根据个别的事实和情况进行判断。

7.31.3 由多个主体组成的集团应识别每个主体的功能货币，以界定那一主体的外币敞口。因此，一个跨国集团内的不同主体通常具有不同的功能货币。该集团作为一个整体并没有功能货币。

7.32 在正常情况下，主体经营所处的主要经济环境就是其主要产生和支出现金的经济环境。[IAS 21 第 9 段]。主体的功能货币通常就是其所在国家的货币，然而也有可能是其他货币。此外，实际情况可能表明境外经营的功能货币与报告主体的功能货币相同。就为了确定功能货币的目的而言，境外经营被定义为经营场所或经营活动在报告主体所在国以外的国家或采用报告主体所使用货币以外的货币的子公司、联营、合营或报告主体的分支机构。[IAS 21 第 8 段]。

7.33 IAS 21 要求主体在确定功能货币时考虑主要指标和次要指标。主要指标是与主体经营所处的主要经济环境密切关联的，因此给予较大的权重。次要指标对于确定主体功能货币提供支持性证据。这两项指标以及需要考虑的因素列示于下表。

功能货币的主要指标 [IAS 21 第 9 段]	
指标	**主体在确定功能货币时需要考虑的因素**
销售和现金流入	(a) *主要影响*商品和劳务销售价格的货币，通常是以该货币进行商品和劳务销售价格的计价和结算。[IAS 21 第 9 (a) (i) 段]。换言之，在主体的产品存在一个当地的活跃销售市场并以当地货币计价且收入主要以该当地货币回款的情况下，该当地货币即为功能货币。然而，准则更着重于决定交易定价的经济环境中的货币，而非交易计价的货币。

ⓒ 2013 普华永道（PricewaterhouseCoopers）版权所有。

Con.

	currency, the local currency is the functional currency. However, the standard gives greater emphasis to the currency of the economy that determines the pricing of transactions than the currency in which transactions are denominated.
	(b) The currency of the country whose competitive forces and regulations *mainly determine* the sales prices of its goods and services. [IAS 21 para 9(a)(ii)]. Where sales prices of the entity's products are determined by local competition and local government regulations rather than worldwide competition or by international prices, the local currency is the functional currency. For example, aircraft manufacturers often price aircraft in US dollars or in euros, but the legal and regulatory environment of the country in which the manufacturer is located may inhibit the entity's ability to pass hard currency costs (that is, dollars or euros) to its customers. Therefore, while the business is influenced by the hard currency, its ability to generate revenue is determined by the local environment, which may indicate that the local currency is the functional currency.
Expenses and cash outflows	The currency that *mainly influences* labour, material and other costs of providing goods and services. This is often the currency in which such costs are denominated and settled. [IAS 21 para 9(b)]. For example, where labour, material and other operating costs are primarily sourced and incurred locally, the local currency is likely to be the functional currency, even though there also might be imports from other countries.
Secondary indicators of functional currency [IAS 21 para 10]	
Indicators	**Factors to be considered by the entity in determining the functional currency**
Financing activities	The currency in which funds from financing activities (for example, issuing debt and equity instruments) are generated. [IAS 21 para 10(a)]. For example, where financing is raised in and serviced by funds primarily generated by the entity's local operation, this may indicate that the local currency is the functional currency, in the absence of other indicators to the contrary.
Retention of operating income	The currency in which receipts from operating activities are usually retained. [IAS 21 para 10(b)]. This is the currency in which the entity maintains its excess working capital balance, which would generally be the local currency.

© 2013 PricewaterhouseCoopers LLP. All rights reserved.

续表

	(b) 各种竞争力量和法规对商品和劳务销售价格起到*主要决定作用*的国家的货币。[IAS 21 9 第(a)(ii)段]。在主体的产品销售价格是由当地的竞争和政府法规决定，而不是由全球竞争和国际价格决定的情况下，该当地货币即为功能货币。例如，飞机制造商们经常采用美元或欧元为飞机定价，但是有些飞机制造商所处国家的法律和监管环境禁止主体将硬通货成本（即美元或欧元）转嫁于其客户。因此，尽管该业务受到硬通货的影响，但其产生收入的能力取决于当地环境，这可能表明当地货币就是功能货币。
费用和现金流出	*主要影响*提供商品和服务所需人工、材料和其他费用的货币，通常以该货币进行此类费用的计价和结算。[IAS 21 第9（b）段]。例如，在人工、材料和其他经营费用主要来源于当地并在当地发生的情况下，该当地货币很可能就是功能货币，即使也可能存在从其他国家进口的情况。
功能货币的次要指标 [IAS 21 第10段]	
指标	**主体在确定功能货币时需要考虑的因素**
融资活动	融资活动（例如，发行债券和权益工具）获得的资金所使用的货币。[IAS 21 第10（a）段]。例如，在融资主要由主体的当地经营所产生的资金中筹集和偿付，且不存在其他相反指标的情况下，这可能表明该当地货币就是功能货币。
经营收入的留存	通常留存从经营活动中收取款项时所使用的货币。[IAS 21 第10（b）段]。这是主体保存多余的营运资本余额所使用的货币，通常可能即为功能货币。

ⓒ 2013 普华永道（PricewaterhouseCoopers）版权所有。

7.34 The above primary and secondary indicators for determining of the functional currency must be considered by all entities. If the entity is a foreign operation, the standard specifies four additional factors that should be considered in determining the functional currency and whether it is the same as that of the reporting entity. These additional factors are shown in the table below. They set out the conditions that point to whether the foreign operation's functional currency is the same as, or different from, the reporting entity (the reporting entity, in this context, being the entity that has the foreign operation as its subsidiary, branch, associate or joint venture).

Additional indicators for foreign operations [IAS 21 para 11]

Indicators	**Conditions pointing to functional currency being *different from* that of the reporting entity**	**Conditions pointing to functional currency being the *same as* that of the reporting entity**
Degree of autonomy	Activities are carried out with a significant degree of autonomy. An example is when the operation accumulates cash and other monetary items, incurs expenses, generates income and arranges borrowings, all substantially in its local currency.	No significant degree of autonomy – activities are carried out as an extension of the reporting entity. An example is when the foreign operation only sells goods imported from the reporting entity and remits the proceeds to it. It follows that such an entity (which would be considered an integral foreign operation in the previous version of IAS 21) must have the same currency as the reporting entity. This is because it would be contradictory for an integral foreign operation that "*carries on business as if it were an extension of the reporting entity's operations*" to operate in a primary economic environment different from its parent. [IAS 21 para BC6].
Frequency of transactions with reporting entity	Few inter-company transactions with the reporting entity.	Frequent and extensive inter-company transactions with the reporting entity.

© 2013 PricewaterhouseCoopers LLP. All rights reserved.

7.34 所有主体必须考虑上述确定功能货币的主要指标和次要指标。如果主体为一个境外经营，准则明确规定在确定其功能货币以及是否与报告主体的功能货币相同时，需要考虑四个补充因素。这些补充因素在下表中列示，其列出了境外经营的功能货币与报告主体的功能货币相同或不同时的情况（这里的报告主体是指拥有该境外经营作为其子公司、分机机构、联营或合营的主体）。

境外经营的补充指标［IAS 21 第 11 段］

指标	**表明功能货币与报告主体功能货币*不同*的情况**	**表明功能货币与报告主体功能货币*相同*的情况**
自主程度	从事业务活动时高度自主。例如，该经营实质上所有的累积现金和其他货币性项目、发生费用、产生收益和安排借款都是以其当地货币进行的。	不具有高度的自主性——从事的业务活动是作为报告主体的延伸。例如，该境外经营仅销售从报告主体进口的商品，并将所得款项汇回报告主体。于是这样的一个主体（在 IAS 21 之前的版本中应该会被认为是构成报告主体经营的组成部分）必须采用与报告主体相同的功能货币。这是因为，对于“*从事的业务如同是报告主体经营的延伸*”的构成整体组成部分的境外经营而言，其是在一个不同于母公司所处的主要经济环境中进行经营应该是存在矛盾的。［IAS 21 第 BC6 段］。
与报告主体进行交易的频率	少量的与报告主体进行公司之间的交易。	大量及频繁的与报告主体进行公司之间的交易。

ⓒ 2013 普华永道（PricewaterhouseCoopers）版权所有。

Con.

Cash flow impact on reporting entity	Mainly in local currency and do not affect reporting entity's cash flows.	Directly impact the reporting entity's cash flows and are readily available for remittance to the reporting entity.
Financing	Primarily in the local currency and serviced by funds generated by the entity's operation.	Significant financing from or reliance on the reporting entity to service existing and normally expected debt obligations.

7.35 The relative importance of the various indicators will vary from entity to entity. For example, the primary and secondary indicators apply to the generality of entities that provide goods and services, but they may not be directly relevant in certain other situations. Examples of situations in which the primary and secondary indicators may be less relevant include treasury entities, structured or special purpose entities, ultimate holding entities and intermediate holding entities. In those situations, management may need to consider the additional indicators stated in paragraph 7.34 above when determining the functional currency.

7.36 In assessing the indicators' relative importance, management may find it useful to consider the following aspects of each indicator:

- The significance of that indicator to the entity's operation. For example, the existence of sterling denominated debt in a foreign entity of a UK parent may not be significant if the foreign entity is primarily self-financing through retained earnings.
- How clearly the indicator identifies a particular currency as the functional currency. For example, if the same entity purchases raw materials both from the UK and locally, the 'expenses' indicator may be inconclusive. In contrast, if the majority of sales occur in the host country at prices determined by local conditions, the 'sales' indicator might be regarded as the key determinant in concluding that the local currency is the functional currency.

7.37 After considering all the factors, the functional currency may still not be obvious. The operation may be diverse, with cash flows, financing and transactions occurring in more than a single currency. In these situations,

© 2013 PricewaterhouseCoopers LLP. All rights reserved.

续表

现金流对报告主体的影响	以当地货币为主，且不影响报告主体的现金流。	直接影响报告主体的现金流，且可以随时汇回报告主体。
融资	以当地货币为主，且由该主体经营活动产生的资金进行偿付。	从报告主体进行重大融资或依赖报告主体偿付现有的或正常预期的债务。

7.35 各种指标的相对重要性随着主体的不同而有所变化。例如，主要指标和次要指标适用于那些提供商品和服务的主体的一般情形下，但在其他某些特定情形下可能并不直接相关。主要指标和次要指标可能具有较低的相关性的例子包括资金业务主体、结构性主体或特殊目的主体、最终控股主体和中间控股主体。在那些情形下，管理层在确定功能货币时可能需要考虑上文第7.34段列出的补充因素。

7.36 在评价各个指标的相对重要性时，管理层可能会发现从下列几个方面来考虑每一个指标是有所帮助的：

- 该指标对于主体经营活动的重要性。例如，如果位于英国的母公司的一个境外经营主要通过留存收益自行融资，那么其以英镑计价的债务可能是不重要的。

- 该指标将某一特定货币识别为功能货币的明确程度。例如，如果同一个主体同时从英国和当地采购原材料，则“费用”指标可能不具有决定性。相反，如果大多数销售发生在主体的所在国家、且销售价格由当地情况所决定，则“销售”指标可能被视为判断当地货币为功能货币的关键决定性因素。

7.37 在考虑了所有因素之后，功能货币可能仍不明显。经营活动可能是多样的，现金流、融资和交易是以一种以上的货币发生。在这些情形下，在确定最能真实地反映相应交易、事项和情况的经济影响的功能货币时需要进行

ⓒ 2013 普华永道（PricewaterhouseCoopers）版权所有。

judgement is required in determining the functional currency that most faithfully represents the economic effects of the underlying transactions, events and conditions. In exercising that judgement, management should give priority to the primary indicators before considering the secondary indicators and the additional factors set out above. [IAS 21 para 12].

7.38 The standard gives greater emphasis to the primary indicators because, as stated above, these indicators are closely linked to the primary economic environment in which the entity operates. The currency of the economy in which the entity operates generally determines the pricing of transactions; this is considered to be more influential than the currency in which the transactions are denominated and settled. This is because transactions can be denominated and settled in any currency management chooses, but as the pricing of the transaction is normally done by reference to the economy of the country whose competitive forces and regulations affect the transaction, the currency of that economy becomes the functional currency by definition. In other words, the currency of the country whose economy drives the business and which determines the gains and losses to be recognised in the financial statements most faithfully reflects the economic effects of the underlying transactions, events and conditions.

7.39 The standard's intention that the primary and secondary indicators should be looked at as a hierarchy is intended to avoid practical difficulties in determining an entity's functional currency. For example, if all the primary indicators, which should be considered together, identify a particular currency as the functional currency, there is no need to consider the secondary indicators. Secondary indicators serve to provide additional supporting evidence in determining an entity's functional currency. [IAS 21 para BC9].

7.39.1 The IFRS IC has considered the functional currency of an ultimate holding entity whose only activity is to hold investments in subsidiaries. In its March 2010 update, it noted that the primary indicators in IAS 21 should not be considered in isolation and that judgement is required when the functional currency is determined. In our view, a policy choice exists for such an ultimate holding entity as to how to interpret IAS 21 in order to determine its functional currency. The ultimate holding entity may determine that it is acting as an extension of its

© 2013 PricewaterhouseCoopers LLP. All rights reserved.

判断。在进行判断时，管理层应当优先考虑主要指标，然后再考虑上文所列出的次要指标和补充因素。[IAS 21 第 12 段]。

7.38　该准则更强调主要指标，这是因为如上文所述，这些指标与主体经营所处的经济环境密切关连的。主体经营所处经济环境的货币通常决定交易的定价；这被认为是比交易的定价和结算货币具有更大的影响。这是因为交易可以以任何管理层选择的货币进行计价和结算，但由于正常情况下交易的定价是参照交易的竞争力和法规的主体所在国家的经济环境，所以根据定义，该经济的货币成为功能货币。换言之，当带动主体业务的是某个国家的经济，并且那个国家的货币决定主体确认在财务报表中的利得和损失时，则那个国家的货币最能真实地反映在该国中的交易、事项和状态的经济影响。

7.39　该准则认为应当按照级次考虑主要和次要指标，以避免在确定主体的功能货币时产生实际操作困难。例如，如果通过整体考虑所有的主要指标可以识别某一特定的货币为功能货币，则无需再考虑次要指标。次要指标的作用是提供确定主体功能货币的补充支持性证据。[IAS 21 结论基础第 9 段]。

7.39.1　IFRS IC 考虑了经营活动仅为控制对子公司的投资的最终控股主体的功能货币。在其 2010 年 3 月的更新中指出，IAS 21 中的主要指标不应当单个孤立地考虑，同时指出在确定功能货币时要求进行判断。我们认为，对于这样一个最终控股主体而言，在如何解读 IAS 21 以确定其功能货币时是存在会计政策选择的。该最终控股主体可能确定其是作为其子公司的延伸，从而采用与那些子公司相同的功能货币。或者由于该主体是一个最终控股主体，其可能考虑 IAS 21 中的“境外经营”指标并未要求其“向下看”而成为是其子

ⓒ 2013 普华永道（PricewaterhouseCoopers）版权所有。

subsidiaries and, therefore, has the same functional currency as those subsidiaries. Alternatively, as the entity is an ultimate holding entity it may consider that IAS 21's 'foreign operation' indicators do not require it to 'look down' and be a foreign operation of its subsidiaries. It is not required to 'look down' simply because there is no entity for the ultimate holding entity to 'look up' to. Under such a view, an entity looks at all of the primary and secondary indicators and will likely conclude that its functional currency is determined by the currency of its own dividend revenue, its own expenses and the currency of its own financing. See further example 3 in paragraph 7.40 below.

7.39.2 When considering the autonomy indicator in paragraph 11 of IAS 21, (see para 7.34 above) typically a non-autonomous subsidiary or branch derives its functional currency from its parent; 'the look up approach' (see example 5 below). For an intermediate holding entity, the autonomy indicator may also point to the conclusion that the intermediate holding entity is acting as an extension of its subsidiary or group of subsidiaries and, therefore, has the same functional currency as its subsidiary or group of subsidiaries; 'the look down approach'. An intermediate holding entity that is not autonomous does not have a policy choice. Whether it is appropriate for such an entity to look up or down depends on the particular facts and circumstances.

7.39.3 Associates and joint ventures are likely to be autonomous from an individual investor given the lack of control in the relationship and the paragraph 11 additional indicators are not likely to be relevant.

Illustrative examples

7.40 Determining an entity's functional currency depends on the facts and circumstances. The following examples are for illustrative purposes only and should not be used as solutions for specific situations.

Example 1 – Functional currency of an entity with transactions denominated in a stable currency.

Example 2 – Functional currency of an entity with products normally traded in a non-local currency (such as oil and gold).

© 2013 PricewaterhouseCoopers LLP. All rights reserved.

公司的一个境外经营。其并未被要求“向下看”只是因为对于该最终控股主体而言，没有主体可供其“向上看”。根据这样一个观点，主体考虑所有主要指标和次要指标，将很可能得出结论，即功能货币根据其自身股利收入和费用的货币以及其自身融资的货币进行确定。进一步参见下文第7.39段中的示例3。

7.39.2　在考虑IAS 21第11段中的自主程度指标时（见上文第7.34段），通常一家非自主的子公司或分支机构的功能货币是来自于其母公司的；即“向上看法”（参见下文示例5）。对于一家中间控股主体而言，自主程度指标可能同样指向这一结论，即中间控股公司是作为其子公司或一组子公司的延伸，因此其功能货币与其子公司或一组子公司的功能货币一致；即“向下看法”。一家非自主的中间控股公司没有会计政策选择。对于这样一个主体，是向上看适当还是向下看适当，这取决于特定的事实和情形。

7.39.3　鉴于某一个别投资者缺乏对于投资关系的控制，联营和合营很可能是自主的，第11段中的补充指标很可能是不相关的。

示例

7.40　确定主体的功能货币取决于事实和情形。以下示例仅作为说明，不应当被用作特定情形的解决方案。

示例1——采用稳定的货币对交易进行计价的主体的功能货币。

示例2——产品（如石油和黄金）通常以非当地货币进行交易的主体的功能货币。

ⓒ 2013 普华永道（PricewaterhouseCoopers）版权所有。

Example 3 – Functional currency of an offshore ultimate holding entity.

Example 4 – Functional currency of an intermediate parent with some operating activities.

Example 5 – Functional currency of an intermediate parent with no operating or financing activities of its own.

Example 6 – Functional currency of an entity raising finance for the group in a foreign currency compared to the other entities in the group.

Example 7 – Functional currency of separate treasury centres in different geographical areas.

Example 8 – Functional currency of a treasury centre that pools resources in the group.

Example 9 – Functional currency of a foreign subsidiary importing products from parent for local distribution.

Example 10 – Functional currency of a structured entity.

Example 11 – Different functional currencies for stand-alone accounts and for group reporting purposes?

Example 12 – Functional currency after a group restructuring.

Example 1 – Functional currency of an entity with transactions denominated in a stable currency

A real estate entity operates in Russia. It owns several office buildings in Moscow and St Petersburg that are rented to Russian and foreign entities. All lease contracts are denominated in US dollars, but payments can be made in either US dollars or in Russian roubles. However, almost all of the lease payments are settled in roubles. This has also been the historical pattern of payment.

On first analysis, the 'sales and cash inflows' indicators appear to produce a mixed response, because the currency that mainly influences the pricing of the lease contracts is the US dollar, whereas the cash inflows are in roubles.

© 2013 PricewaterhouseCoopers LLP. All rights reserved.

示例 3——海外最终控股主体的功能货币。

示例 4——附有一些经营活动的中间母公司的功能货币。

示例 5——本身没有经营或融资活动的中间母公司的功能货币。

示例 6——以不同于集团内其他主体所使用的货币为集团募集外币资金的主体的功能货币。

示例 7——位于不同地理区域的单独资金中心的功能货币。

示例 8——统筹集团资源的资金中心的功能货币。

示例 9——从母公司进口产品以在当地销售的境外子公司的功能货币。

示例 10——结构性主体的功能货币。

示例 11——独立报表和出于集团报告目的的报表采用不同的功能货币？

示例 12——集团重组后的功能货币。

示例 1——采用稳定的货币对交易进行计价的主体的功能货币

一家在俄罗斯经营的房地产主体，在莫斯科和圣彼得堡拥有若干办公大楼，出租给俄罗斯和境外主体。所有租赁合同都以美元计价，但付款可以采用美元或者俄罗斯卢布。然而，几乎所有的租赁付款都是以卢布进行结算的，这也是历史结算方式。

首先分析，“销售和现金流入”指标似乎给出了一个混合的回应，因为主要影响租赁合同定金的货币是美元，而现金流入则是卢布。此外，诸如主要经营成本、不动产管理、保险、税项和员工成本等现金流出很可能

ⓒ 2013 普华永道（PricewaterhouseCoopers）版权所有。

Also, cash outflows such as the principal operating costs, management of properties, insurance, taxes and staff costs are likely to be incurred and settled in roubles, which would indicate that the functional currency is the Russian rouble.

The lease payments are denominated in US dollars, but the US dollar is not considered to be significant to the entity's operation because: (a) most of the collection is in roubles, which is subject to short-term changes in US dollar/rouble exchange rate; and (b) it is the local conditions and circumstances in Russia, not the US, that determine the rental yields of properties in Moscow and St Petersburg that mainly influence the pricing of the lease contracts, which are merely denominated in US dollar.

It is, therefore, the currency of the Russian economy, rather than the currency in which the lease contracts are denominated, that most faithfully represents the economic effects of the real estate activity in Russia. Since the transactions are denominated in a different currency to the entity's functional currency, there is an embedded foreign exchange derivative in the contract that may have to be separated in as explained in paragraph AG33 (d) of IAS 39. For further guidance on embedded derivatives refer to chapter 5 of IFRS Manual of Accounting – Financial Instruments.

Example 2 – Functional currency of an entity with products normally traded in a non-local currency (such as oil and gold)

Entity A operates an oil refinery in Saudi Arabia. All of the entity's income is denominated and settled in US dollars. The oil price is subject to the worldwide supply and demand, and crude oil is routinely traded in US dollars around the world. Around 45% of entity A's cash costs are imports or expatriate salaries denominated in US dollars. The remaining 55% of cash expenses are incurred in Saudi Arabia and denominated and settled in riyal. The non-cash costs (depreciation) are US dollar denominated, as the initial investment was in US dollars.

The functional currency of entity A is the US dollar. The crude oil sales prices are influenced by global demand and supply. Crude oil is globally traded in US dollars around the world. The revenue analysis points to the US dollar.

© 2013 PricewaterhouseCoopers LLP. All rights reserved.

是以卢布产生并结算的，这些应该会表明功能货币是俄罗斯卢布。

租赁付款是以美元计价，但对于主体的经营而言，美元并不被认为是重大的，因为：（a）大多数款项是以卢布收回的，这受到美元对卢布汇率的短期变动的影响；（b）决定位于莫斯科和圣彼得堡的不动产的租赁收益、并对租赁合同定价产生主要影响的是俄罗斯当地的情况和环境，而非美国，这些租赁合同仅仅是以美元计价。

因此，俄罗斯经济的货币是最能真实反映俄罗斯境内房地产活动的经济影响的，而不是这些租赁合同的计价货币。由于这些交易是以不同于该主体功能货币的另一种货币计价的，租赁合同中包含一个按照 IAS 39 AG 第 33（d）段说明的、可能必须分离的嵌入外币衍生工具。有关嵌入衍生工具的进一步指引，请参见《国际财务报告准则实务指引——金融工具系列》第五章。

示例 2——产品（如石油和黄金）通常以非当地货币进行交易的主体的功能货币

主体 A 在沙特阿拉伯经营一家炼油厂，其所有收益均以美元计价和结算。油价受全球供需的影响，原油在全球范围内循例以美元进行交易。主体 A 的现金成本中约有 45% 为以美元计价的进口或外籍职工薪酬，其余 55% 的现金费用在沙特阿拉伯发生，以里亚尔进行计价和结算。由于初始投资为美元，非现金成本（折旧）以美元计价。

主体 A 的功能货币为美元。原油的销售价格受全球供需影响，其在全球范围内以美元进行交易。收入分析指向美元，而成本分析则是混合的。由于主要经济环境是主体产生和支出现金所处的环境，所以折旧（或其

ⓒ 2013 普华永道（PricewaterhouseCoopers）版权所有。

The cost analysis is mixed. Depreciation (or any other non-cash expenses) is not considered, as the primary economic environment is where the entity generates and expends cash. Operating cash expenses are influenced by the riyal (55%) and the US dollar (45%). Management is able to determine the functional currency as the US dollar, as the revenue is clearly influenced by the US dollar and expenses are mixed.

Example 3 – Functional currency of an offshore ultimate holding entity

A group of companies is organised as follows:

Entity A is a reporting entity with three operating subsidiaries (entities B, C and D) that are incorporated in Russia. Management has concluded that the functional currency of each subsidiary should be the local currency (roubles).

Entity A is the holding entity and has been set up by institutional investors in Cyprus (a eurozone country). Entity A has obtained equity and loan financing and has invested in Russian entities B, C and D. It pools cash from all group entities, invests excess cash and obtains external financing, according to the group's needs. The financing is drawn in US dollars, and all of its monetary assets are denominated in US dollars. The entity retains cash in US dollars, its expenses that are not associated with financing are insignificant compared to the investments in the Russian investees or the funding costs and it has no employees. The entity's activities are carried out by employees of its operating subsidiaries. Its shares are denominated in US dollars and it pays dividends to its investors in US dollars.

In January 2010, the IFRS IC received a request for guidance on determining the functional currency of an ultimate investment holding entity. The IFRS IC was asked whether the underlying economic environment of its subsidiaries should be considered in determining the functional currency of an ultimate investment holding company. The IFRS IC decided not to issue guidance on this matter, but noted that assessing functional currency requires the exercise of judgement and that the paragraph 9 indicators (sales and expenses) should not be considered in isolation. Our view is that there is an accounting policy choice for determining the functional currency of an ultimate holding entity in

© 2013 PricewaterhouseCoopers LLP. All rights reserved.

他非现金费用）不予考虑。经营现金费用受里亚尔（55%）和美元（45%）的影响。由于收入明显受美元影响，而费用受到混合影响，所以管理层能够确定其功能货币为美元。

示例 3——海外最终控股主体的功能货币

一个集团公司由如下组成：

主体 A 为报告主体，有三家设立于俄罗斯的经营子公司（主体 B、主体 C 和主体 D）。管理层已经得出结论，每一家子公司的功能货币应为当地货币（卢布）。

主体 A 为控股主体，由几个机构投资者在塞浦路斯（一个欧元区国家）设立。主体 A 已经取得了权益投资和贷款融资，并投资于俄罗斯的主体 B、主体 C 和主体 D。其从集团内各个主体汇集现金，并根据集团的需求将多余的现金进行投资或从外部取得融资。获取的融资为美元，其所有的货币性资产均以美元计价。该主体保留美元现金，与对于俄罗斯被投资方的投资和集资成本相比，主体发生的与融资不相关的费用是不重大的。主体没有职工，其活动是由其经营子公司的职工来执行的。主体 A 的股份是以美元计价的，并以美元向其投资者支付股利。

2010 年 1 月，IFRS IC 收到了一个请求，要求就确定最终投资控股主体的功能货币提供指引。IFRS IC 被问及在确定一家最终投资控股公司的功能货币时是否应当考虑其子公司所涉及的经济环境。IFRS IC 决定不就此事项发布指引，但指出评价功能货币要求进行判断、并且第 9 段中的指标（销售和费用）不应当孤立地考虑。我们的观点是，在此情形下确定最终控股主体的功能货币是存在会计政策选择的：

ⓒ 2013 普华永道（PricewaterhouseCoopers）版权所有。

this situation:

Option 1: The ultimate holding entity is viewed as having the same functional currency as its operating subsidiaries. Entity A's functional currency is the Russian rouble.

Management is required to use its judgement to determine the functional currency that most faithfully represents the economic effects of the underlying transactions, events and conditions. [IAS 21 para 12]. Entity A has no activity of its own. The currency that reflects the economic substance of the underlying economic events that affect the holding entity is the Russian rouble, as all of the holding entity's subsidiaries operate in Russia and entity A's primary source of income will be dividends obtained from the subsidiaries in Russia. Entity A's ability to service debts and pay dividends to shareholders is dependent on the Russian economy. Although paragraph 11 of IAS 21 explicitly defines a foreign operation as a reporting entity's subsidiary, branch, associate or joint venture, paragraph 11 may be applied by analogy, and viewing an ultimate investment holding entity as an extension of its subsidiaries is appropriate.

Option 2: The ultimate holding entity's functional currency is not viewed as being dependent on its foreign operations. Entity A's functional currency is the US dollar.

Entity A has no sales or purchases, nor does it incur significant expenses other than in respect of its financing activities. The economic source of dividend revenues is not a key factor in determining the functional currency of a non-operating ultimate parent entity. The primary indicators in paragraph 9 are not directly relevant. It is the currency denomination of the financing activities that drives the functional currency determination (the secondary indicators in paragraph 10). The functional currency is determined based on the primary economic environment in which the entity generates and expends cash, consistent with the secondary indicators. All cash flows associated with financing and dividends are US dollar. Paragraph 11 of IAS 21 explicitly defines a foreign operation as a reporting entity's subsidiary, branch, associate or joint venture. While a foreign operation may be viewed as an extension of

© 2013 PricewaterhouseCoopers LLP. All rights reserved.

选择1：该最终控股主体被视为与其经营子公司拥有相同的功能货币。主体 A 的功能货币为俄罗斯卢布。

管理层被要求运用其判断，以确定最能真实地反映所涉及的交易、事项和情况的经济影响的功能货币。[IAS 21 第 12 段]。主体 A 自身并没有经营活动。由于该控股主体所有的子公司均在俄罗斯运营，所以反映影响该控股主体的相关经济事项的实质的货币是俄罗斯卢布。主体 A 偿付债务和向股东支付股利的能力取决于俄罗斯经济。虽然 IAS 21 第 11 段明确将一个境外经营定义为一个报告主体的子公司、分支机构、联营或合营，但是可能通过类比运用第 11 段，所以将最终投资控股主体视作其子公司的延伸是适当的。

选择2：不将该最终控股主体的功能货币视为依赖于其境外经营。主体 A 的功能货币为美元。

主体 A 没有销售或采购，除了融资活动外也没有发生其他重大费用。在确定一个非经营性最终母公司的功能货币时，股利收入的经济来源不是一个关键因素。第 9 段中的主要指标不是直接相关的。推动功能货币确定的是融资活动的计价货币（第 10 段中的次要指标）。功能货币的确定是基于主体产生和支出现金所处的经济环境，这与次要指标一致。所有与融资和股利相联系的现金流均为美元。IAS 21 第 11 段明确将境外经营定义为一个报告主体的子公司、分支机构、联营或合营。尽管一个境外经营可能被视作其母公司的延伸，但是第 11 段并没有要求运用类比将一个最终投资控股主体视作其子公司的延伸，这是因为母公司控制子公司，而子公司并不控制母公司。

ⓒ 2013 普华永道（PricewaterhouseCoopers）版权所有。

its parent, paragraph 11 is not required to be applied by analogy to view an ultimate investment holding entity as an extension of its subsidiary, because the parent controls the subsidiary and not *vice versa.*

Example 4 – Functional currency of an intermediate parent with some operating activities

Parent (entity P) is a manufacturing business located in the UK with sterling as the functional currency. Entity P invests US dollars in an intermediate parent (entity IP), which then invests in three separate US dollar operating subsidiaries (entity S1, S2 and S3). Entity IP undertakes no 'operating' activities of its own; however, it acts as the holding entity of the US subsidiaries – heading up the US group. It has a dedicated management team and staff that carry out the head office functions, including the US group's payroll, cash management and preparation of a sub-consolidation package. The management team takes finance decisions related to the sub-group and controls the activities of the sub-group. Its management team reports monthly to entity P's board on the results of the US group. Its key cash inflows are the dividends from its subsidiaries (which it remits up directly to entity P), and inter-company balances from its subsidiaries (that are used to settle both entity IP's own administration costs and those costs incurred directly by entity IP on behalf of its subsidiaries – that is payroll costs, computer services, maintenance, etc). All cash inflows and outflows are denominated in US dollar. Entity IP is a US-registered entity.

Entity IP has operating activities, in that it provides local management services to its subsidiaries. It incurs local costs and then either recharges these to its subsidiaries or retains dividend income from its subsidiaries to pay for these costs. All the costs incurred are incurred in US dollar and will be reimbursed in US dollar.

Entity IP does not raise finance; consideration of the currency in which funds from financing activities are generated is not directly applicable. However, the funding of its costs through dividends and inter-company balances is in US dollars. The currency in which receipts from operating activities is usually retained indicates a US dollar functional currency.

© 2013 PricewaterhouseCoopers LLP. All rights reserved.

示例4——附有一些经营活动的中间母公司的功能货币

母公司（主体P）是一个位于英国的制造业务，其功能货币为英镑。主体P将美元投资于一家中间母公司（主体IP），随后主体IP又投资于三家单独的以美元运营的子公司（主体S1、主体S2和主体S3）。主体IP本身不承担“经营”活动；然而，其是作为美国子公司的控股主体——领导美国集团。主体IP拥有专职的管理团队和人员来行使总部职能，包括美国集团的工资、现金管理和子合并包的编制。该管理团队作出与子集团相关的财务决策、控制子集团的经营活动，并每月向主体P的董事会报告美国集团的经营成果。主体IP的主要现金流为来自其子公司的股利（其将股利直接汇给上级主体P）和来自其子公司的公司之间往来款（这些余额是用来结算主体IP自身的管理费用和主体IP替其子公司直接发生的费用，即工资费用、计算机服务费、维护费等）。所有的现金流入和流出均以美元计价。主体IP为一家在美国注册的主体。

主体IP有经营活动，即向其子公司提供当地管理服务。其在当地发生费用，然后向其子公司收取或留存来自其子公司的股利收入以支付这些费用。所有发生的费用均为美元，并将以美元偿付。

主体IP并不进行融资；考虑融资活动产生的资金所使用的货币并不直接适用。然而，通过股利和公司之间往来款以支付其费用的资金为美元。通常留存从经营活动中收取款项时所使用的货币表明其功能货币为美元。

ⓒ 2013 普华永道（PricewaterhouseCoopers）版权所有。

Looking to the additional factors in paragraph 11 of IAS 21 revised:

- Entity IP has a significant degree of autonomy: it has its own management team and staff; a budget for which it is responsible; and discretion over its head office functions.
- It has a number of transactions with parties outside the group.
- The cash flows of entity IP do not directly affect the parent; entity IP is not merely acting as a conduit.

Consideration of paragraph 11(d), '*whether cash flows from activities of the foreign operation are sufficient to service existing and normally expected debt obligations without funds being made available by the reporting entity*' is not applicable.

Unlike example 5, entity IP is carrying out operating activities of its own, albeit not in the traditional trading sense. These activities consist of holding and managing the subsidiaries of the sub-group. Under paragraphs 9 and 10 of IAS 21 revised, the costs entity IP incurs and any receipts retained from operating activities are in US dollar. IP in this example is not merely acting as a conduit/'cash box' for entity P. It is carrying out management activities and has a significant degree of autonomy. It has an active management team and exercises discretion over the US group's operations. The US group has been structured in this way for operational as well as tax reasons. This suggests that entity IP's functional currency is not necessarily that of entity P. The functional currency of entity IP would be US dollar.

Example 5 – Functional currency of an intermediate parent with no operating or financing activities of its own

Parent (entity P) is a manufacturing business located in the UK with sterling as the functional currency. P invests US dollar in an intermediate parent (entity IP), which then invests in a US-dollar operating subsidiary (entity S) on behalf of entity P. Entity IP is a shell entity that undertakes no operating or financing activities as it only holds investments. Its key cash inflows are dividends from entity S, which it remits directly to parent entity P. Entity IP

© 2013 PricewaterhouseCoopers LLP. All rights reserved.

来看看 IAS 21 第 11 段中的补充因素：

- 主体 IP 具有高度自主：其有自己的管理团队和员工、由其负责的预算、以及行使总部职能的自主权。

- 其与集团外的各方有许多交易。

- 主体 IP 的现金流不直接影响母公司；其不仅仅是作为一个“过道”。

对第 11（d）段的考虑，即“*在报告主体不提供资金的情况下，境外经营活动所产生的现金流是否足够偿付现有及正常预期的债务*”是不适用的。

与示例 5 不同，主体 IP 是在开展自身的经营活动，尽管不是传统贸易意义上的经营活动。这些活动包括对子集团内的各个子公司进行控股和管理。根据修订后的 IAS 21 第 9 和第 10 段，主体 IP 发生的成本和从经营活动中留存的款项均为美元。本例中的主体 IP 不仅仅是作为主体 P 的一个过道或是“现金保管箱”；其确实在开展管理活动，拥有高度自主权，同时还拥有活跃的管理团队，并对美国集团的营运自主决策。以这种方式设置美国集团有经营方面和税务方面的原因，这间接表明主体 IP 的功能货币并不必定是主体 P 的功能货币。主体 IP 的功能货币应该是美元。

示例 5——本身没有经营或融资活动的中间母公司的功能货币

母公司（主体 P）是一个位于英国的制造业务，其功能货币为英镑。主体 P 将美元投资于一家中间母公司（主体 IP），随后主体 IP 又代表主体 P 投资于一家功能货币为美元的经营子公司（主体 S）。由于主体 IP 仅持有投资，所以其是一家不从事经营或融资活动的壳主体。其主要现金流入是来自于主体 S 的股利，其会将该股利直接汇给母公司主体 P。主体 IP 为一家在美国注册的主体。

ⓒ 2013 普华永道（PricewaterhouseCoopers）版权所有。

is a US-registered entity.

Entity IP undertakes no operating or financing activities. Any investing activity that entity IP undertakes is not carried out as a separate stand-alone activity, but at the behest of its parent. It is not, therefore, relevant to consider the 'sales and cash inflow' indicator. The 'expenses and cash outflow' indicator may be relevant, as it is more likely than not that entity IP will incur some local costs. But that indicator by itself is not considered significant to entity IP's operations, nor does it clearly identify the US dollar as the functional currency.

The secondary indicators do not clearly identify the US dollar as the functional currency, as entity IP does not raise any finance from external local sources – any finance raised is primarily from its parent or from sterling sources. Nor does entity IP retain any funds for own use, which are all remitted to the parent. All the additional factors also point to the US dollar not being the currency that most faithfully represents entity IP's activities of receiving dividend income from entity S in US dollar and remitting these to its parent.

The primary, secondary and additional indicators are mixed and therefore management should exercise judgement in determining the currency that most faithfully represents entity IP's activities.

One analysis might focus on the fact that Entity IP is a 'foreign operation' in relation to its parent, entity P. entity IP does not have autonomy, transacts frequently with its parent and does not retain cash and relies on parent P for financing. It is, therefore, simply a device or a shell corporation for the holding of investments that could have been held by entity P itself. The functional currency of entity IP is the same as its parent: sterling.

An alternative analysis might focus on the fact that the results of entity IP are dependent on the economic activities of its subsidiary whose functional currency is the US dollar. The cash inflow indicator, therefore, suggests that the US dollar is significant to its investing activity.

The facts and circumstances indicate that entity IP is a shell intermediate holding entity that merely holds the investment and receives occasional

© 2013 PricewaterhouseCoopers LLP. All rights reserved.

主体 IP 不从事经营或融资活动，其从事的任何投资活动都不是作为一个单独的活动进行的，而是执行母公司的指令。因此，考虑“销售和现金流入”指标是不相关的。“费用和现金流出”指标可能是相关的，因为主体 IP 很可能将在当地发生一些费用；但是该指标本身对于主体 IP 的经营而言不认为是重大的，也不能明确地识别美元为功能货币。

由于主体 IP 不从当地外部渠道进行融资，其融资主要是通过其母公司或英镑来进行的，所以次要指标也不能明确地识别美元为功能货币。主体 IP 也不会留存任何资金供自身使用，而是将所有资金汇给母公司。所有补充因素也都指向美元不是最能真实地反映主体 IP 活动（从主体 S 取得美元股利收益并汇给其母公司）的货币。

主要指标、次要指标和补充指标是混合的，因此管理层应当运用判断以确定最能真实反映主体 IP 经营活动的货币。

一种分析可能着重于主体 IP 是一家与其母公司（主体 P）相关的“境外经营”这一事实。主体 IP 不具有自主性，与其母公司交易频繁，不留存现金，并且依靠主体 P 进行融资。因此，主体 IP 仅是一个为控股而设立的装置或壳公司，这本可以由主体 P 自己完成。所以主体 IP 的功能货币应与其母公司一致，即英镑。

或者另一种分析可能着重于主体 IP 的经营成果取决于其功能货币为美元的子公司的经济活动这一事实。因此，现金流入指标间接表明美元对于其投资活动而言是重大的。

事实和情形表明主体 IP 是一个中间控股壳公司，仅持有投资、偶尔收取股利并上缴给母公司。由于主体 IP 是根据母公司的指令设立并营运的，

ⓒ 2013 普华永道（PricewaterhouseCoopers）版权所有。

dividends, passing them on to the parent. Entity IP does not have autonomy as it was set up and operates at the behest of the parent, carrying out a function that the parent could equally carry out itself. Our view is that sterling is entity IP's functional currency.

Example 6 – Functional currency of an entity raising finance for the group in a foreign currency compared to the other entities in the group

A French-listed parent has significant French, UK and US operating subsidiaries, but no Japanese operations. The French parent creates a new subsidiary, Newco SA, incorporated and resident in France. Newco issues in yen 1bn of equity capital to French parent, receiving yen 1bn of cash. Newco also raises yen 100m of external financing and places the yen 1.1bn total cash on deposit with a bank in Japan, earning 0.1% interest per annum. The cash will be reinvested in yen-denominated financial instruments such as bonds and commercial paper. Newco has few staff that manages the entity's investing activities. It incurs sterling operational costs that are insignificant compared to the interest paid on its yen borrowing. Like any wholly-owned subsidiary, the retained profits are under the parent's control.

Newco does not undertake any key operating activities on its own. Consideration of the currency that mainly influences sales and costs is not directly relevant. Newco incurs expenses in euro, but these are not significant enough to suggest that the euro is the functional currency. It is necessary to look at the secondary indicators.

Newco raises finance by issuing its own equity instruments to the parent in a currency that is different from the parent, but the proceeds are invested in yen-denominated assets at the behest of the parent. The external funds raised through the issue of debt instruments are insignificant compared to the issue of equity shares to the parent. The question is silent as to whether the income generated from the investments is reinvested in other yen denominated assets or whether it is wholly passed on to the parent. Whatever that may be, the decision to reinvest or distribute is under the parent's control.

Consideration of the other additional factors suggests that Newco is a 'cash

© 2013 PricewaterhouseCoopers LLP. All rights reserved.

其不具有自主性，其行使母公司自身也同样能够行使的职能。我们的观点是，英镑为主体 IP 的功能货币。

示例 6——以不同于集团内其他主体所使用的货币为集团募集外币资金的主体的功能货币

一家在法国上市的母公司在法国、英国和美国拥有重大的经营子公司，但在日本没有经营机构。法国母公司创建了一家新的子公司（新公司 SA），其注册及经营场所位于法国。新公司向法国母公司发行了 10 亿日元的股本，收到 10 亿日元现金。新公司还通过外部融资取得资金 1 亿日元，并将总计 11 亿日元的现金存入日本的一家银行，赚取年利率为 0. 1% 的利息。该现金将会被再投资于以日元计价的金融工具，诸如债券和商业票据。新公司只有少数负责管理主体投资活动的职员。其发生的英镑营运成本，相对于其日元借款所支付的利息而言是不重大的。如同所有全资子公司一样，新公司的留存收益由母公司控制。

新公司本身不从事任何关键经营活动。对于主要影响销售和成本的货币的考虑是不直接相关的。新公司发生的费用为欧元，但这些并不足够重大以间接表明欧元为功能货币。因此需要考虑次要指标。

新公司通过向母公司发行自身的权益工具来融资，取得了与母公司货币不同的外币资金，但是收到的款项是按照母公司的指示投资于以日元计价的资产。通过发行债务工具取得的资金与通过向母公司发行股份取得的资金相比是不重大的。本示例对于投资产生的收益是再投资于其他以日元计价的资产还是全部上缴给母公司，并未作出说明。无论是哪种可能，再投资或分配的决定都是受母公司控制的。

对其他补充因素的考虑间接表明新公司是一个“现金保管箱”类型的主

ⓒ 2013 普华永道（PricewaterhouseCoopers）版权所有。

box' type entity with no independent management/activity. Newco is simply a conduit for the parent entity that could invest the yen directly. It may be that the only reason the parent entity has invested the yen through Newco is in the hope that its exposure to changes in the euro/yen exchange rate is reported in other comprehensive income through the translation of its net investment in Newco, rather than in the income statement, which would be the case if the yen deposits were treated as belonging to the parent. The 'autonomy factor' points to the euro as the functional currency, as Newco appears to be merely an extension of the activities of the parent. This would point to the functional currency being the same as that of its parent – the euro. This would be the answer if Newco carried out only the activities described.

The investing activity could have been done by the parent rather than the subsidiary and, therefore, based on the additional indicators relevant to a foreign operation, the parent's functional currency should determine the foreign entity's functional currency.

Example 7 – Functional currency of separate treasury centres in different geographical areas

A Swiss multi-national entity with Swiss franc as its functional currency has operating subsidiaries in the US and Europe whose functional currencies are the US dollar and the euro respectively. It has established a treasury centre (TC) in each of these geographical regions. The activities of the two TCs are identical in that each provides financial and risk management services to its relevant operating subsidiaries. All transactions (for example, management of liquid funds, borrowings and hedging activities) between a TC and its respective operating subsidiaries are carried out either in US dollars or euros.

Each TC earns dividends and income from cash management activities in US dollars and euros respectively. Each TC charges a monthly fee for providing such financial services to its operating subsidiaries that is denominated either in US dollars or euros, depending on its area of operation. All operating costs – such as staff costs payable to treasury and financial management specialists and other administrative and running costs – are incurred and settled by each TC in US dollars or euros. The TCs' short and long-term financing are

© 2013 PricewaterhouseCoopers LLP. All rights reserved.

体，没有独立的管理/经营活动。新公司仅仅是母公司能够直接投资日元的一个过道。母公司主体通过新公司进行日元投资的唯一原因可能是希望通过对其在新公司的净投资的折算而将欧元对日元的汇率变动敞口计入其他综合收益，而不是计入利润表（如果日元存款属于母公司就应该是这样处理）。由于新公司似乎仅仅是母公司经营活动的一个延伸，所以“自主因素”指向欧元为功能货币。这应该会指向新公司的功能货币与其母公司一致，即欧元。如果新公司仅执行所述活动，则其功能货币应该是欧元。

此投资活动本可以由母公司完成，而不通过其子公司，因此基于与境外经营相关的补充指标，该母公司的功能货币应当决定该境外主体的功能货币。

示例 7——位于不同地理区域的单独资金中心的功能货币

一家以瑞士法郎作为其功能货币的跨国主体在美国和欧洲有多家经营子公司，这些子公司的功能货币分别为美元和欧元。该主体在每一个地理区域都设立了资金中心，这两个资金中心的经营活动完全一样，即向各自相关的经营子公司提供金融和风险管理服务。资金中心与各自经营子公司之间的所有交易（例如流动资金、借款和套期活动的管理）均以美元或欧元进行。

每个资金中心从管理活动中分别赚取以美元和欧元计价的股利和收益。每个资金中心于每月向其经营子公司为其所提供的金融服务收取报酬，并根据其经营区域分别以美元或欧元计价。所有经营成本——诸如支付给现金和财务管理专业人员的职工成本和其他行政营运成本——由每个资金中心分别以美元或欧元发生和结算。资金中心的短期和长期融资是由瑞士母公司以瑞士法郎贷款形式提供的。资金中心不留存任何从其经营活动中产生的美元或欧元供自身使用，扣除当地发生的费用后，管理

ⓒ 2013 普华永道（PricewaterhouseCoopers）版权所有。

provided by the Swiss parent in the form of Swiss franc loans. The TCs do not retain any US dollars or euros generated from their operation for their own use. After meeting local expenses, management either uses US dollars or euros to settle the inter-entity payables to the operating subsidiaries or distributes any surplus to the parent as dividends.

This response addresses only the US dollar TC; the considerations for the euro TC are the same.

The primary factors (currency that influences sales price and the costs of providing goods and services) are arguably irrelevant because TC does not have any third-party sales and purchases. However, the determination of the functional currency is an entity-by-entity question and it is not relevant to whether an entity's fee income comes from inside or outside the group. What is relevant is the nature of the fee income and the manner in which it is earned. In this example, the TC provides financial services to the US operating subsidiaries for which it charges a fee. The fees are invoiced and settled in US dollar. TC also earns investment income in US dollars. As TC earns its revenue and income in US dollar and the underlying US economy determines the pricing of TC's fee income to the US operating subsidiaries, the 'sales and cash inflow' indicator identifies the US dollar as the functional currency of TC. As all administrative and local expenses are incurred and settled in US dollar, the 'expenses and cash outflow' indicator also provides strong evidence that the US dollars is the TC's functional currency. The primary economic environment in which the TC generates and expends cash is the US and, therefore, its functional currency is the US dollar.

The primary indicators are clear, so there is no need to consider the secondary indicators, even if these seem to provide evidence that the Swiss franc is the functional currency (for example, TC's short and long-term financing is primarily in the form of Swiss franc loans from the parent).

Example 8 – Functional currency of a treasury centre that pools resources in the group

A UK multi-national entity with sterling as its functional currency has set up a

© 2013 PricewaterhouseCoopers LLP. All rights reserved.

层会用剩余美元或欧元支付经营子公司的内部应付款项或将所有余款作为股利分配给母公司。

以下讨论只针对使用美元的资金中心；对使用欧元的资金中心应同样考虑。

由于资金中心不存在与第三方的销售和采购，所以有理由认为主要因素（影响销售价格及提供商品和服务成本的货币）是不相关的。然而，功能货币的确定是一个关于单个主体的问题，与主体的酬金收入是来自于集团内部还是集团外部是不相关的，相关的是酬金收入的性质和赚取的方式。本示例中资金中心向美国经营子公司提供金融服务并收取报酬，该报酬以美元开具发票并结算。资金中心也以美元赚取投资收益。由于资金中心以美元赚取其收入和收益、且其所处的美国经济决定了其对美国经营子公司的酬金收入的定价，所以“销售和现金流入”指标识别美元为资金中心的功能货币。由于所有管理和当地的费用均以美元发生并结算，“费用和现金流出”指标也提供了很强的证据证明美元是该资金中心的功能货币。资金中心产生和支出现金所处的主要经济环境为美国，因此其功能货币为美元。

主要指标很明确，因此即使次要指标似乎显示瑞士法郎为功能货币（例如，资金中心的短期和长期融资主要是由瑞士母公司以瑞士法郎贷款形式提供的），也无须予以考虑。

示例8——统筹集团资源的资金中心的功能货币

一家以英镑作为其功能货币的英国跨国主体在瑞士设立了一个资金中心。

ⓒ 2013 普华永道（PricewaterhouseCoopers）版权所有。

treasury centre (TC) in Switzerland. TC borrows US dollars, euros and sterling in the euro-market and lends the proceeds to its parent and other operating subsidiaries with the loans denominated in the borrowing entity's functional currency. As part of its cash management operations, it pools the liquid resources of the parent and the operational units and invests them temporarily in the euro-market. It also manages foreign exchange and interest rate risks of operating units by executing derivative contracts with third parties and/or with operating units.

TC earns dividends and income from cash management activities in US dollar, euros and sterling. It charges a monthly fee for providing such financial services to its parent and operating subsidiaries that is denominated in the relevant entity's functional currencies. All operating costs, such as staff costs payable to treasury and financial management specialists and other administrative and running costs are incurred and settled in Swiss francs. TC's short and long-term financing needs are provided by its parent in the form of sterling loans.

TC provides financial services to group companies for which it charges a fee. However, the fees are invoiced in the functional currencies of the group companies and settled in those currencies. This ensures that the risk of non-functional currency transaction gains and losses on all inter-company transactions with the TC are passed on from the operating units to the TC for centralised management and control. TC also earns investment income in US dollar, euro and sterling. As TC earns its revenue and income in different currencies, the 'sales and cash inflow' indicator fails to identify a particular currency that is significant in its own right as the functional currency of TC. Furthermore, there is no explicit or implicit evidence to suggest that the underlying Swiss economy determines the pricing of TC's fee income to the group companies.

On the other hand, as all administrative and local expenses are incurred and settled in Swiss francs, the 'expenses and cash outflow' indicator provides strong evidence that Swiss franc is the functional currency.

Therefore, as the primary indicators are not sufficiently conclusive in

© 2013 PricewaterhouseCoopers LLP. All rights reserved.

资金中心在欧元市场上借入美元、欧元和英镑，并将取得的资金借给其母公司和其他经营子公司，该贷款以借款方的功能货币进行计价。作为现金管理营运的一部分，该资金中心统筹母公司和各经营单位的流动资源，并将其暂时投资于欧元市场。其也通过与第三方和/或其他经营单位执行衍生工具合同，对各经营单位的外汇和利率风险进行管理。

资金中心从美元、欧元和英镑的现金管理活动中赚取股利和收益。对于向其母公司和经营子公司提供的此类金融服务，资金中心每月收取以各相关主体功能货币计价的报酬。所有营业成本，诸如应付资金和金融管理专家的职工成本、其他管理和营运成本均以瑞士法郎发生并结算。资金中心的短期和长期融资需求均由其母公司以英镑贷款的形式提供。

资金中心向集团公司提供金融服务，同时收取报酬。然而，该报酬是以集团公司的功能货币开具发票并结算的。这保证所有与资金中心非功能货币的公司间交易的汇兑损益风险都从各经营单位转移到资金中心，以便集中管理控制。资金中心也赚取美元、欧元和英镑的投资收益。由于资金中心赚取不同币种的收入和收益，“销售和现金流入”指标无法识别某一自身重大的特定货币作为资金中心的功能货币。另外，没有明示或隐含的证据间接表明其所处的瑞士经济决定了资金中心向各集团公司收取的酬金收入的定价。

另一方面，由于所有管理和当地费用都以瑞士法郎发生并结算，因此“费用和现金流出”指标为瑞士法郎为功能货币提供了有力的证据。

所以，当主要指标不足以决定性地识别功能货币时，需要考虑次要指标。

ⓒ 2013 普华永道（PricewaterhouseCoopers）版权所有。

identifying the functional currency, it is necessary to consider the secondary indicators.

The secondary indicators provide evidence that sterling is the functional currency. This is because TC does not raise any finance from external local sources for meeting the cost of its operations in excess of its operating income but relies on short- and long-term financing from its parent. Furthermore, since cash inflows from operations occur in various currencies that are used to meet local expenses, retention of cash indicator is not significant in determining TC's functional currency.

The additional factors also support sterling as the functional currency. For example, the 'autonomy indicator' suggests that the UK parent has set up the TC to achieve overall financial efficiency of its international operations through centralised control and effective management of cash and financial risk. The volume of inter-company transactions is large due to the regular transfer of foreign currency cash balances from and to the parent. The cash flows of the TC, therefore, impact the parent's cash flows on a regular basis. The financing indicator also identifies sterling as the functional currency.

This analysis suggests that the primary indicators do not provide conclusive evidence that the local currency of the country in which TC operates is its functional currency. However, the secondary indicators support sterling as the functional currency. Overall, the evidence is mixed. Management should exercise judgement in determining the currency that most faithfully represents the economic effects of TC's activities. There are a number of possible solutions. One indicator may be that TC has been set up primarily as a conduit to undertake the treasury operations of the entire multi-national group headed by the UK parent. The currency of the country that most faithfully represents TC's operations is, therefore, the functional currency of the UK parent: sterling. Another factor to consider is whether any of the three major currencies (dollars, euros, sterling) is dominant. If no clear currency is suggested by the previous factors, and if the TC's operating expenses are significant, the Swiss franc may be the TC's functional currency.

© 2013 PricewaterhouseCoopers LLP. All rights reserved.

次要指标提供了英镑为功能货币的证据。这是因为对于超出经营收益的营运成本部分，资金中心并未从外部当地资源取得融资，而是依赖其母公司的短期和长期融资。另外，由于用以弥补当地费用的经营现金流入是以多个币种发生的，所以现金留存指标对于确定资金中心的功能货币而言是不重大的。

补充因素同样支持英镑作为功能货币。例如，“自主指标”间接表明英国母公司设立该资金中心旨在通过对现金和财务风险进行集中控制和有效管理，以达到国际业务整体财务效率的目标。公司之间的大量交易是因为外币现金余额的定期流出和流入母公司；因此，资金中心的现金流会定期影响母公司的现金流。融资指标也识别出英镑为功能货币。

这一分析间接表明主要指标没有提供决定性的证据，以证明资金中心经营所处的国家的当地货币为其功能货币。然而，次要指标支持英镑作为功能货币。总之，证据的指向是混合的。管理层在确定最能真实反映资金中心活动的经济影响的货币时应当进行判断。可能存在几个解决方案。一项指标可能是资金中心的设立主要是作为一个过道，以承担整个由英国母公司领导的跨国集团的资金营运；因此，最能真实反映资金中心营运的货币是英国母公司的功能货币，即英镑。另一个需考虑的因素是三种主要货币（美元、欧元和英镑）中是否有一种货币占主导。如果前述因素都不能清楚地表明功能货币，并且如果资金中心的营业费用是重大的，那么瑞士法郎可能是该资金中心的功能货币。

ⓒ 2013 普华永道（PricewaterhouseCoopers）版权所有。

Example 9 – Functional currency of a foreign subsidiary importing products from parent for local distribution

A subsidiary located in Spain imports a product manufactured by its US parent at a price denominated in US dollars. The product is sold throughout Spain at prices denominated in euros, which are determined primarily by competition with similar locally produced products. All selling and operating expenses are incurred locally and paid in euros. The operation's long-term financing is primarily in the form of US dollar loans from the parent. The distribution of profits is under the parent's control.

The 'sales and cash inflows' indicators suggest that the foreign subsidiary's functional currency is the euro, as that is the currency in which the sales prices are denominated and settled. Furthermore, the sales prices for the foreign entity's products do not respond on a short-term basis to changes in exchange rates, but are determined by local competition and local government regulation. This is a strong indicator that the functional currency is the euro.

The 'expenses and cash outflows' indicators provide a mixed response. This is because cost of sales is primarily denominated and settled in US dollars, whereas local expenses, including selling expenses, are denominated and settled in euros. Given that a significant part of the expenses are settled in US dollars, this indicator does not provide conclusive evidence that the euro is the functional currency.

The primary indicators produce a mixed response, although overall they favour the euro. It is, therefore, necessary to look at the secondary indicators.

The secondary indicators provide supporting evidence that US dollar is the functional currency. This is because the foreign subsidiary's long-term financing is primarily in the form of US dollar loans from the parent, and the subsidiary does not raise any finance from external local sources. Furthermore, the foreign subsidiary does not retain any euros generated from its operations for its own use. After meeting local expenses, management either uses the euros to settle the inter-entity payables to the parent, or

© 2013 PricewaterhouseCoopers LLP. All rights reserved.

示例 9——从母公司进口产品以在当地销售的境外子公司的功能货币

一家位于西班牙的子公司进口一种由其美国母公司生产的产品，其价格以美元计价。该产品在整个西班牙进行销售，其价格以欧元计价。价格主要由与当地生产的同类产品之间的竞争情况进行确定。该子公司所有的销售和经营费用都在当地发生且以欧元支付。该经营的长期融资主要是以母公司提供美元贷款的形式。利润分配受母公司控制。

由于销售价格是以欧元计价并结算的，所以“销售和现金流入”指标间接表明该境外子公司的功能货币为欧元。此外，该境外主体的产品的销售价格不受短期汇率变动的影响，而是由当地竞争和当地政府法规决定。这是欧元为功能货币的有力指标。

“费用和现金流出”指标提供的反馈是混合的，这是因为销售成本主要以美元计价和结算，而包括销售费用在内在当地费用以欧元计价和结算。考虑到费用的重大部分是以美元结算的，所以这项指标不能提供欧元是功能货币的决定性证据。

虽然这些主要指标总体上倾向于欧元，但是其给出的反馈是混合的。因此，需要考虑次要指标。

各次要指标为美元是功能货币提供了支持性的证据。这是因为，该境外子公司的长期融资主要是以母公司提供美元贷款的形式，其自身并不从外部当地资源取得融资。另外，该境外子公司不留存任何从经营活动中产生的欧元供自身使用。在扣除在当地发生的费用之后，管理层会将剩余欧元用于向母公司支付内部应付款项，或将所有余款作为股利分配给母公司。

ⓒ 2013 普华永道（PricewaterhouseCoopers）版权所有。

distributes any surplus to the parent as dividends.

If the 'autonomy' indicator suggests that the foreign subsidiary is simply acting as an agent for its US parent by selling parent-produced goods to customers in Spain, collecting the proceeds and remitting the same to the US parent, the functional currency would be US dollar. The volume of inter-company transactions is large, as the foreign subsidiary imports goods from its US parent and settles the proceeds on a regular basis. The subsidiary's cash flows, therefore, regularly impact the parent's cash flows.

However, if the foreign subsidiary's operations were carried out with a significant degree of autonomy (that is, local management has a significant degree of authority and responsibility, such as to borrow loans, invest excess cash, modify prices or grant discounts and hire and fire staff), the functional currency would be determined independently from the parent. Management would conclude that the functional currency is the euro, as the primary indicators of paragraph 9 of IAS 21 are overall in favour of the euro.

Example 10 – Functional currency of a structured entity

Entity A is a US bank with a US dollar functional currency. Entity A establishes a structured entity in a European country in order to invest in a European bond portfolio. Entity A has funded the structured entity with equity and inter-company debt denominated in euros. The structured entity uses the financing to purchase a portfolio of euro government bonds. There is no intention for the structured entity to perform any activities other than holding the bond portfolio. The directors are all employees of the US parent, and the structured entity has no active management of its own.

The functional currency of the structured entity is the US dollar, as the entity has no operations and does not provide any services. The primary indicators, therefore, do not apply. The 'financing' indicator supports the euro, as all financing is in euros. However, all the financing is inter-company and entity A could denominate the financing in any currency it wanted. Considering the 'autonomy' indicator, it is clear the structured entity is not autonomous. It is a shell entity, has no independent activities and no active management of its own.

© 2013 PricewaterhouseCoopers LLP. All rights reserved.

如果“自主”指标间接表明该境外子公司仅仅是其美国母公司的代理，负责向西班牙客户销售母公司生产的商品以及收取货款并将其汇回美国母公司，其功能货币应该是美元。由于该境外子公司定期从美国母公司进口商品及结算货款，所以公司间的交易量较大；因此，该子公司的现金流也会定期地影响母公司的现金流。

然而，如果该境外子公司从事经营活动具有高度自主（即，当地管理层在诸如借款、投资多余现金、调整价格或授予折扣以及职工任免等方面具有高度自主和重大责任），其功能货币的确定应该是独立于母公司的。由于 IAS 21 第 9 段中的主要指标总体上倾向于欧元，管理层应该可以得出功能货币是欧元的结论。

示例 10——结构性主体的功能货币

主体 A 是一家美国银行，以美元为功能货币。主体 A 在一个欧洲国家设立了一个结构性主体，以对某欧洲债券资产组合进行投资。主体 A 以欧元计价的股权投资和公司间债权的方式为结构性主体提供资金。该结构性主体使用该融资额购买欧元政府债券组合。除持有债券组合外，该结构性主体没有开展其他业务活动的意图。该结构性主体的所有董事均为其美国母公司的职工，且其自身没有活跃的管理层。

由于该主体没有业务活动，也不提供任何服务，所以该结构性主体的功能货币为美元；因此，主要指标不适用。由于所有融资均为欧元，“融资”指标支持欧元为功能货币；然而，所有融资均为公司间的、且主体 A 可以根据其意愿使用任何货币进行计价。至于“自主”指标，显然该结构性主体并非自主经营，而是一个壳公司，既没有独立的业务活动，也没有其自身活跃的管理层。

© 2013 普华永道（PricewaterhouseCoopers）版权所有。

Example 11 – Different functional currencies for stand-alone accounts and for group reporting purposes?

Entity A is an autonomous foreign operation of reporting entity Z. Entity A operates in a country where the US dollar is frequently used because the local currency has been inflationary in the past.

Entity A primarily operates in the local market and is requested to prepare statutory standalone financial statements in accordance with IFRS. Local regulations require entity A to use the local currency as presentation currency for the statutory accounts. Management has determined that the local currency should be the functional currency for the standalone financial statements. Entity A is also required to prepare an IFRS reporting package for entity Z. Management believes that entity A should use the US dollar as the functional currency for group reporting purposes, because the US dollar is frequently used in the local economy and because the group presentation currency is the US dollar.

An entity can have only one functional currency. The functional currency is the currency of the primary economic environment. This is the same for standalone financial statements and group reporting purposes. Entity A should use the local currency as its functional currency for both statutory and group reporting purposes.

Example 12 – Functional currency after a group restructuring

Group X is a complex multinational group with numerous intermediate parent entities. As part of a group restructuring, intermediate parent entity A sold some of its subsidiaries to intermediate parent company B. Should the functional currency of both entities, A and B, be re-assessed after the group restructuring?

Yes. The functional currency of both companies should be re-assessed to determine whether the previous IAS 21 functional currency determination is impacted by the group restructuring. For example, if the subsidiaries sold to entity B are substantial operating companies and entity B has limited or no other activities, IAS 21 may require entity B to have the same functional

© 2013 PricewaterhouseCoopers LLP. All rights reserved.

示例 11——独立报表和出于集团报告目的的报表采用不同的功能货币？

主体 A 是报告主体 Z 的自主境外经营。主体 A 经营所处的国家通常使用美元，这是因为当地货币过去一直是通货膨胀的。

主体 A 主要在当地市场进行经营，并且被要求按照 IFRS 编制独立的法定财务报表。当地法规要求主体 A 对于法定报表使用当地货币作为列报货币。管理层已经决定当地货币应当是其独立财务报表的功能货币。主体 A 还被要求为主体 Z 编制一套 IFRS 的编报材料。管理层认为，主体 A 应使用美元作为其功能货币进行集团编报工作，因为当地经济中通常使用美元且集团的列报货币为美元。

一个主体只能有一个功能货币。功能货币是主要经济环境的货币，这对于编制独立财务报表和进行集团编报而言是一样的。主体 A 应当使用当地货币作为其功能货币进行法定及集团编报工作。

示例 12——集团重组后的功能货币

集团 X 是一家拥有多个中间母公司的综合性跨国集团。作为集团重组的一部分，中间母公司 A 将其部分子公司出售给了中间母公司 B。在集团重组后，公司 A 及公司 B 是否应对各自的功能货币进行重新评价？

是的。两家公司均应对其功能货币进行重新评价，以确定集团重组是否对之前根据 IAS 21 确定的功能货币产生了影响。例如，如果出售给主体 B 的这些子公司拥有规模较大的经营，而主体 B 仅开展有限的业务活动或者根本没有其他业务活动，则 IAS 21 可能会要求主体 B 采用其新购买的子公司的功能货币作为自己的功能货币。另一方面，公司 B 可能是作

ⓒ 2013 普华永道（PricewaterhouseCoopers）版权所有。

currency as that of the newly acquired subsidiaries. On the other hand, entity B may be acting as an extension of its ultimate parent entity X, in which case the functional currency will be the same as that of entity X both before and after the group restructuring. The group restructuring by itself does not trigger a reassessment of the functional currency of the ultimate holding entity X, because nothing has changed as regards to the primary economic environment in which the holding company operates. The functional currency of X would have been determined before by X's management according to the policy choice in example 3, and the ultimate holding entity X may or may not have independent activities. The existence or not of such activities does not determine whether an intermediate holding entity is an extension of its parent.

Entity with multiple operations

7.41 The definition of a foreign operation indicates that an operation should have activities. [IAS 21 para 8]. An entity might have more than one distinct and separable operation, such as a division or a branch. In determining whether each operation may be considered a separate entity for the purposes of this standard, the definition of a 'business' per IFRS 3 could be useful. For example, a foreign entity might have one operation that acts as a selling agent, receiving inventories of goods from the parent entity and remitting the proceeds back to the entity, and another operation that manufactures and sells products locally. If those two operations are conducted in different economic environments, they may have different functional currencies.

7.42 Once the number of operations has been determined, each foreign entity should determine its functional currency and measure its results and financial position in that currency before it can be included in the reporting entity when it prepares its financial statements. Once the foreign entity's functional currency is determined, the results and financial position of its branches having different functional currencies will be included in the foreign entity using the translation method set out in paragraph 7.83 below.

© 2013 PricewaterhouseCoopers LLP. All rights reserved.

为其最终母公司 X 的延伸，在那样的情况下，不论在集团重组之前或之后，主体 B 的功能货币将与主体 X 的功能货币一致。集团重组本身并不会触发对于最终控股主体 X 的功能货币的重新评价，这是因为该控股公司经营所处的主要经济环境没有发生改变。主体 X 的功能货币应该在重组之前已经由其管理层根据示例 3 中的会计政策选择进行了确定，而该最终控股主体 X 可能拥有也可能没有独立的业务活动。是否存在此类活动并不能决定一家中间控股公司是否是其母公司的延伸。

多元经营的主体

7.41　境外经营的定义表明一个经营应当要有业务活动。[IAS 21 第 8 段]。一个主体可能拥有一个以上的独特的及可分离的经营，诸如一个部门或一个分支机构。在确定一项经营是否可以被视为该准则下的一个单独主体时，IFRS 3 对“业务”的定义可能是有帮助的。例如，一个境外主体可能有一项经营是作为销售代理，从母公司收取存货商品并将货款汇回母公司；有另一项经营是在当地生产和销售产品。如果那两个经营是在不同的经济环境中开展业务活动，其可能会有不同的功能货币。

7.42　一旦确定了经营的数量，每一个境外主体应当确定其功能货币，并在其被包含在报告主体所编制的财务报表之前，应当以该功能货币计量其经营成果和财务状况。境外主体的功能货币一旦确定，其具有不同功能货币的分支机构的经营成果和财务状况将按照下文第 7.83 段所列出的折算方法并入该境外主体。

© 2013 普华永道（PricewaterhouseCoopers）版权所有。

Different functional currencies for entities in the same country

7. 43 It is also possible for an entity to have two or more foreign operations in one country and determine different functional currencies for those entities. For example, a UK entity could have a sales branch and an operating subsidiary in the same country, which justifies different functional currencies. Another example is where the UK entity has a subsidiary in a foreign country that manufactures and sells goods locally, and another subsidiary in that same country whose operations are fundamentally different. Management should determine for each of these entities the appropriate functional currency using the guidance addressed in paragraph 7. 31 above.

Accounting records not maintained in functional currency

7. 44 If a foreign operation's books or records are not maintained in its functional currency, management should remeasure into the functional currency. That remeasurement is required at the time the foreign operation prepares its financial statements before they are translated into the presentation currency of the reporting entity. The remeasurement into the functional currency, which should be carried out using the translation method set out in paragraph 7. 48 onwards below, would produce the same amounts in the functional currency as would have occurred had all the items been recorded in the functional currency in the first place. For example, monetary items are translated into the functional currency using the closing rate, and non-monetary items that are measured on a historical cost basis are translated using the exchange rate at the date of the transaction that resulted in their recognition. [IAS 21 para 34].

Change in functional currency

7. 45 Once the functional currency of an entity is determined, it should be used consistently, unless significant changes in economic facts, events and conditions indicate that the functional currency has changed. For example, a branch that

© 2013 PricewaterhouseCoopers LLP. All rights reserved.

位于同一国家内的多个主体具有不同的功能货币

7.43 一个主体也可能在一个国家拥有两个或两个以上的境外经营，并确定那些主体具有不同的功能货币。例如，一个英国主体可能在同一国家拥有一家销售分支机构和一家经营子公司，并且证明其拥有不同的功能货币。另一个例子是英国主体在境外国家有一家在当地生产和销售商品的子公司，在同一个国家有另一家经营活动完全不同的子公司。管理层应当采用上文第 7.31 段阐述的指引以确定各主体的适当的功能货币。

未采用功能货币记账的会计记录

7.44 如果一个境外经营的账簿或记录未以其功能货币进行记录，管理层应当以功能货币进行重新计量。要求在该境外经营编制财务报表时，在其财务报表折算为报告主体的列报货币以前，进行重新计量。重新计量为功能货币应当采用列示于第 7.48 段及其下文的折算方法，其产生的以功能货币列示的金额应该会与这些项目从一开始就以功能货币记录形成的结果一致。例如，货币性项目按照期末汇率折算为功能货币，以历史成本计量的非货币性项目按照导致其进行确认的交易日的汇率折算。[IAS 21 第 34 段]。

功能货币的变更

7.45 一个主体的功能货币一旦确定，其应当一致地使用，除非经济事实、事项和状态发生的重大变化表明其功能货币已经改变。例如，一家作为报告主体业务延伸的分支机构，可能由于情形的改变而成为一家本质上独立的、

ⓒ 2013 普华永道（PricewaterhouseCoopers）版权所有。

carried out its operations as an extension of the reporting entity's business may become independent and primarily regional in nature as a result of changed circumstances.

7.46 A change in functional currency should be accounted for *prospectively* from the date of change. In other words, management should translate all items (including balance sheet, income statement and statement of comprehensive income items) into the new functional currency using the exchange rate at the date of change. [IAS 21 para 37]. Because the change was brought about by changed circumstances, it does not represent a change in accounting policy and, therefore, a retrospective adjustment under IAS 8 is not relevant. As all items are translated using the exchange rate at the date of change, the resulting translated amounts for non-monetary items are treated as their historical cost. There is no specific guidance in IAS 21 on what should be done with equity items, but it would be consistent that these are also translated using the exchange rate at the date of the change of functional currency. This means that no additional exchange differences arise on the date of the change.

7.46.1 Entities should also consider presentation currency (see further para 7.76) when there is a change in functional currency. It may be that the presentation currency does not change. For example, a standalone Irish entity previously presented its financial statements in its euro functional currency and its functional currency changes to US dollar. It is based in Ireland and has Irish shareholders. It does not wish to change its presentation currency and so continues to present its financial statements in euros. Alternatively, the entity is part of a group and the presentation currency of the group does not change following the change in functional currency of a foreign operation. In such a case the numbers in the entity's own financial statements for the period up to the change in functional currency do not change in presentational currency terms. From the point that the functional currency changes new foreign exchange differences will arise in the entity's own financial statements when items expressed in the new functional currency are translated into the presentation currency.

7.46.2 An example follows of an entity changing its functional but not its presentation currency.

© 2013 PricewaterhouseCoopers LLP. All rights reserved.

主要是地区性的主体。

7.46　功能货币的变更应当自变更之日起采用未来适用法进行会计处理。换言之，管理层应当采用变更日的汇率将所有项目折算为新的功能货币（包括资产负债表、利润表和综合收益表项目）。[IAS 21 第 37 段]。因为该变更是由环境的改变而引起的，其并不作为会计政策的变更，所以与 IAS 8 要求的追溯调整是不相关的。由于所有项目均采用变更日的汇率进行折算，产生的非货币性项目折算后的金额视为其历史成本。IAS 21 未提供应当如何处理权益项目的具体指引，但对于权益项目同样采用变更功能货币之日的汇率进行折算应该是与 IAS 21 的原则一致的。这就意味着变更当日不会产生额外的汇兑差异。

7.46.1　当功能货币发生变更时，主体也应当考虑列报货币（参见第 7.76 段的进一步讨论）。列报货币可能没有发生变更。例如一个独立的爱尔兰主体，之前以其功能货币欧元列报其财务报表，随后其功能货币变更为美元。该主体位于爱尔兰，并有爱尔兰的股东，所以其并不希望改变其列报货币，故继续以欧元列报其财务报表；或者，该主体是某个集团的一部分，该集团的列报货币并未随着境外经营功能货币的变更而变更。在这种情况下，截至功能货币变更前期间的主体自身财务报表中以列报货币列示的数字不会发生改变。而自功能货币变更时点后，当以新功能货币表示的项目折算为列报货币时，该主体自身的财务报表中产生新的外币折算差额。

7.46.2　下文是一个主体变更功能货币但未变更列报货币的例子。

ⓒ 2013 普华永道（PricewaterhouseCoopers）版权所有。

Example 1 – Change in functional currency

Using the Irish entity example from paragraph 7.46.1, assume that its functional currency changes to US dollars on 1 January 20X8. The entity presented its financial statements for the year to 31 December 20X7 in euros. It will continue to present its 20X8 financial statements in euros. In its 20X8 financial statements, its 20X7 comparatives will be exactly as they were in the 20X7 financial statements. A US dollar loan, for example, will be translated into euro at the closing rate, with exchange differences between opening and closing rates recorded in the income statement. An item of property, plant and equipment (PP&E) that was purchased in euro will be stated at its euro historical cost less depreciation.

On 1 January 2008 all financial statement items are translated into US dollars at the rate ruling at that date.

In its 20X8 financial statements, no foreign exchange will arise on the US dollar loan in the entity's 20X8 income statement, as it is now an item expressed in the entity's functional currency. Any monetary items that are not denominated in US dollars will be translated at the closing rate with exchange differences recorded in the income statement.

Any items of PPE will have been retranslated into US dollars at 1 January 20X8 and these retranslated amounts become their US dollar historical cost and accumulated depreciation (see further para 7.46.3). The PPE is depreciated in US dollars throughout 20X8.

In the entity's separate financial statements, CTA will be recognised in other comprehensive income and recorded in a separate component of equity. CTA is reclassified to profit or loss on disposal of a foreign operation (see further para 7.106). In the context of the entity's separate financial statements where there is one functional currency and a different presentation currency, the 'foreign operation' is the entire business of the entity. CTA would, therefore, only ever be reclassified if the entire business of the entity were to be sold, leaving a shell.

© 2013 PricewaterhouseCoopers LLP. All rights reserved.

示例1——功能货币的变更

以第7.46段的爱尔兰主体为例，假设其功能货币于20X8年1月1日变更为美元。该主体以欧元列报其截至20X7年12月31日的财务报表。其将继续以欧元列报其20X8年的财务报表。在其20X8年财务报表中，其20X7年的比较数据将与其在20X7年财务报表中的数据完全一致。例如，一笔美元贷款将以期末汇率折算为欧元，相应的期初与期末间的汇兑差额计入利润表。以欧元购入的不动产、工厂和设备项目（PP&E）将以其欧元历史成本减去折旧列示。

于20X8年1月1日，所有财务报表项目均以当日汇率折算为美元。

在其20X8年财务报表中，该主体的20X8年利润表中将不会产生该美元贷款的汇兑差额，因为此时该美元贷款是以主体的功能货币进行表示的项目。任何未以美元计价的货币性项目将会以期末汇率进行折算，其汇兑差额将计入利润表。

不动产、工厂和设备的任何项目将于20X8年1月1日被重新折算为美元，并且这些重新折算后的金额即为其美元历史成本和累计折旧（参见第7.46.3段的进一步讨论）。该项目在整个20X8年中皆以美元计提折旧。

在该主体的单独财务报表中，累计折算调整将确认于其他综合收益，并记录为权益的一个单独组成部分。处置一项境外经营时，累计折算调整应被重分类至损益（参见第7.106段的进一步讨论）。在主体的单独财务报表有一种功能货币和另一种不同的列报货币的情况下，该“境外经营”就是该主体整个业务。因此，如果该主体的整个业务将被出售，即剩下一个壳时，累计折算调整应该会被重分类。

© 2013 普华永道（PricewaterhouseCoopers）版权所有。

7.46.3 In the case where a foreign entity such as a subsidiary is translated into a different presentation currency, cumulative translation adjustment (CTA) will arise in the presentation currency consolidated financial statements. When the functional currency of that foreign entity changes, to one that may be the same or different from the group's presentation currency, any CTA previously recorded in equity remains in equity and is only adjusted on disposal or part-disposal of the foreign entity. [IAS 21 para 37]. For disposals and partial disposals see paragraph 7.106.

7.46.4 A change in functional currency may be accompanied by a change in presentation currency, as many entities prefer to present financial statements in their functional currency. Accounting for a change in presentation currency is dealt with from paragraph 7.82 below. A change in presentation currency is accounted for as a change in accounting policy and is applied retrospectively, as if the new presentation currency had always been the presentation currency.

Example 1 – Change in functional currency: impact on a depreciated asset

A UK entity has a branch in France with a sterling functional currency. The UK entity presents its financial statements in sterling. A significant change in trading operations and circumstances occurred during the first quarter of the financial year ended 30 June 20X6. This meant that sterling no longer faithfully represents the underlying transactions, events and conditions of the foreign branch. UK management decided that the euro should be the functional currency of its foreign operation and that all transactions undertaken from the beginning of the financial year 30 June 20X6 (that is, from 1 July 20X5) should be recorded in euros.

The branch purchased, on 1 January 20X0, an asset for € 164,000 with a useful life of 10 years; the rate of exchange was £1 = € 1.64. Since the branch's functional currency was sterling, the asset is recorded at the sterling equivalent cost of £100,000. At 1 July 20X5, the equipment has a net book value of £50,000.

As a result of the change in functional currency from sterling to euros on 1 July 20X5 (exchange rate at 30 June 20X5 is £1 = € 1.45), the functional

© 2013 PricewaterhouseCoopers LLP. All rights reserved.

7.46.3　在境外主体（诸如一家子公司）被折算成不同的列报货币的情形下，在以列报货币列示的合并财务报表中将会产生累计折算调整（CTA）。当该境外主体的功能货币变更为与集团的列报货币相同或不同的货币时，之前计入权益的CTA仍保留在权益中，仅在该境外主体被处置或部分处置时进行调整。[IAS 21 第 37 段]。

7.46.4　由于很多主体倾向于以其功能货币列报财务报表，所以功能货币的变更可能伴随着列报货币的变更。列报货币变更的会计处理将在下文第 7.82 段中阐述。列报货币的变更是作为会计政策变更进行处理的，并采用追溯调整法，如同新的列报货币一直就是列报货币。

示例 1——功能货币的变更：对折旧资产的影响

一个英国主体在法国有一个以英镑为功能货币的分支机构，该英国主体以英镑列报其财务报表。在截至 20X6 年 6 月 30 日财务年度的第一季度中，境外分支机构的贸易经营和环境发生了重大变化。这意味着英镑不再能真实地反映该境外分支机构的交易、事项和状态。英国管理层确定了，欧元应当是其境外经营的功能货币，并且从 20X6 年 6 月 30 日财务年度开始（即从 20X5 年 7 月 1 日开始）的所有交易均应当以欧元记录。

该分支机构于 20X0 年 1 月 1 日以 164,000 欧元购买了一项使用寿命为 10 年的资产；汇率为 1 英镑 = 1.64 欧元。由于当时该分支机构的功能货币为英镑，该资产以 100,000 英镑的等值成本入账。于 20X5 年 7 月 1 日，该设备的账面净值为 50,000 英镑。

由于该分支机构的功能货币自 20X5 年 7 月 1 日起由英镑变更为欧元（20X5 年 6 月 30 日的汇率为 1 英镑 = 1.45 欧元），该资产的功能货币金

ⓒ 2013 普华永道（PricewaterhouseCoopers）版权所有。

currency amount of the asset is carried at is € 72,500 (£50,000 @ 1.45, presented as cost of € 145,000 and accumulated depreciation of € 72,500). This becomes its new historical net book value.

If the asset had been expressed in euro since its purchase it would have had a net book value of € 82,000 (€ 164,000 × 5/10). This number is only relevant if, as a result of exchange movements, the new historical net book value exceeded the previous historical euro value at the date of change. In such a case an impairment review could be necessary if the indications are that the recoverable amount is less than € 82,000 and the asset is carried at more than € 82,000. [IAS 21 para 25].

The financial statements of the euro branch will be retranslated into sterling from the date that its functional currency changed to euro, and CTA will arise from this point on the difference between opening net assets at opening versus closing rates, and profit or loss at average to closing rates, where the UK entity presented, and continues to present, its financial statements in sterling.

If the UK entity decided to change its presentation currency to euro for its 30 June 20X6 financial statements, it would need to go through the process described in paragraph 7.82 below in order to present its sterling functional currency branch in euro for prior periods. This involves translating the assets and liabilities at the closing rate at 30 June 20X4 and translating the income statement at actual or average rates for year to 30 June 20X5. Equity items should be translated at historic or closing rates, and retained earnings and CTA should be restated if practicable to do so. From 1 July 20X5 no retranslation will be required in relation to the euro branch, since the euro branch has the same functional currency as the UK entity's presentation currency. The sterling to euro CTA that is calculated up to 30 June 20X5 will remain in equity until the branch is disposed of or subject to partial disposal.

7.47 It may not be practicable to determine the date of change precisely at a point during the year. It is also likely that the change may have occurred gradually during the year. If so, it may be acceptable to account for the change as of the beginning or end of the accounting period in which the change occurs, whichever more closely approximates the date of change.

© 2013 PricewaterhouseCoopers LLP. All rights reserved.

额变为 72,500 欧元（50,000 英镑 ×1.45，以成本 145,000 欧元和累计折旧 72,500 欧元进行列报），此金额即为该资产新的历史账面净值。

如果该资产自购买之日起即以欧元表示，其账面净值应该会是 82,000 欧元（164,000 欧元 × 5/10）。这一金额仅在汇率变动导致新的历史账面净值大于之前以欧元表示的变更日的历史价值时才具有相关性。在这种情形下，如果有迹象表明该资产的可收回金额小于 82,000 欧元而资产却以大于 82,000 欧元的金额载于账上，则可能需要对该资产进行减值复核。[IAS 21 第 25 段]。

在英国主体以英镑并继续以英镑列报其财务报表的情况下，该欧元分支机构的财务报表自其功能货币变更为欧元之日起将会被重新折算为英镑，并且从这一时点起，期初净资产按照期初汇率和期末汇率之间的差额以及损益按照平均汇率和期末汇率的差额将产生 CTA。

如果该英国主体决定将 20X6 年 6 月 30 日的财务报表的列报货币变更为欧元，其应该会需要通过如下文第 7.82 段所描述的流程，从而将以英镑为功能货币的分支机构的以前期间数据以欧元进行列报。这涉及以 20X4 年 6 月 30 日的期末汇率折算资产和负债以及以实际汇率或截至 20X5 年 6 月 30 日的年度平均汇率折算利润表。权益项目应当以历史汇率或期末汇率进行折算，如果可行，留存收益和 CTA 应当予以重述。由于自 20X5 年 7 月 1 日起，该欧元分支机构的功能货币与英国主体的列报货币相同，该分支机构无需进行重新折算。至 20X5 年 6 月 30 日由英镑折算为欧元而产生的 CTA 将保留在权益中，直至该分支机构被处置或部分处置。

7.47 精确地确定年度期间中的某个时点为变更日可能是不切实可行的，变更也很可能是在年度期间中逐渐发生的。如果是这样，以变更所发生的会计期间的期初或期末（哪个更接近于变更日）对变更进行会计处理可能是可接受的。

ⓒ 2013 普华永道（PricewaterhouseCoopers）版权所有。

Example 1 – Change in functional currency

The facts are the same as in the previous example; a UK entity has a branch in France with sterling as its functional currency. A significant change in trading operations and circumstances occurred during the first quarter of the financial year ended 30 June 20X6. This meant that sterling no longer faithfully represented the underlying transactions, events and conditions of the foreign branch. The UK management decided that the euro should be the functional currency of its foreign operation and that all transactions undertaken from the beginning of the financial year 30 June 20X6 should be recorded in euros.

The foreign branch's financial statements at 30 June 20X5, previously prepared in sterling, are translated to euros at the rate of exchange ruling at the date of change – in this situation, 1 July 20X5, the first day of the current financial year. All items in the balance sheet are translated at the rate of exchange ruling at 30 June 20X5, which approximates to the date of change. Retrospective application is not permitted, as the change in functional currency is accounted for prospectively.

Foreign currency transactions

Introduction

7.48 Foreign currency transactions are transactions denominated in a currency other than the entity's functional currency. Foreign currency transactions may produce receivables or payables that are fixed in terms of the amount of foreign currency that will be received or paid. For example, an entity may buy or sell goods or services in a foreign currency; borrow or lend money in a foreign currency; acquire or dispose of assets; or incur and settle liabilities in a foreign currency.

© 2013 PricewaterhouseCoopers LLP. All rights reserved.

示例 1——功能货币的变更

事实背景与之前的例子相同；一个英国主体拥有一家位于法国的、功能货币为英镑的分支机构。在截至 20X6 年 6 月 30 日财务年度的第一季度中，该分支机构的贸易经营和环境发生了重大变化。这意味着英镑不再能真实地反映该境外分支机构的交易、事项和状态。英国管理层决定，欧元应当是其境外经营的功能货币，并且从 20X6 年 6 月 30 日财务年度开始的所有交易均应当以欧元记录。

该境外分支机构之前以英镑编制的 20X5 年 6 月 30 日财务报表，按变更日的汇率折算为欧元。本示例中的变更日即为 20X5 年 7 月 1 日（当期财务年度的第一天）。资产负债表中的所有项目均按 20X5 年 6 月 30 日（即近似于变更日）的汇率折算。功能货币的变更采用未来适用法进行会计处理，不允许采用追溯调整法。

外币交易

引言

7.48　外币交易是指以主体功能货币以外的货币计价的交易。外币交易可能产生将来收取或支付以固定外币金额计价的应收或应付款项。例如，一个主体可能买入或者卖出以外币计价的商品或者劳务；借入或者借出外币资金；购买或者处置资产；或者以外币发生或结算负债。

ⓒ 2013 普华永道（PricewaterhouseCoopers）版权所有。

Initial recognition

7.49 A foreign currency transaction is recorded, on initial recognition in the functional currency, by applying to the foreign currency amount the spot exchange rate between the functional currency and the foreign currency at the date of the transaction. [IAS 21 para 21]. This process is known as 'translation' – financial data denominated in one currency is expressed in terms of another currency. Translation includes not only the expression of individual transactions in terms of another currency, but also the expression of a complete set of financial statements prepared in one currency in terms of another currency (see para 7.76).

7.50 The date of transaction is the date on which the transaction first qualifies for recognition in accordance with IFRS. [IAS 21 para 22]. The spot exchange rate is the exchange rate for immediate delivery. [IAS 21 para 8]. For revenues, expenses, gains and losses, the spot exchange rate at the dates on which those elements are recognised is used. Translation at the actual exchange rate at the dates the numerous revenues, expenses, gains and losses are recognised is generally impractical; management may, therefore, use a rate that approximates to the actual rate – for example, an average rate.

7.51 The above requirements appear straightforward, but their application may create problems. They include: determining the date of transaction, which may not always be obvious; determining an average rate as an approximation to the actual rate; and the selection of an appropriate rate for translating foreign currency transactions where there is more than one rate in operation.

Determining the average rate

7.52 Management may use an average rate for a period for recording foreign currency transactions as a proxy to the actual rate prevailing at the date of each transaction, provided that there is no significant change in rates during that period. An average rate is unlikely to be used by entities undertaking few transactions in a foreign currency. It is also unlikely to be used for translating large, one-off transactions that would be recorded at the actual rate. The flexibility allowed in IAS 21 is likely to be most beneficial to entities that enter into a large number of

© 2013 PricewaterhouseCoopers LLP. All rights reserved.

初始确认

7.49 外币交易在初始确认时以功能货币记录，按交易发生日功能货币和外币之间的即期汇率进行折算。［IAS 21 第 21 段］。这一过程被称为“折算”，即用一种货币来表示以另一种货币计价的财务数据。折算不仅包括将个别的交易以另一种货币表示，也包括将以一种货币编制的一整套财务报表以另一种货币表示（参见第 7.76 段）。

7.50 交易发生日是指交易首次符合 IFRS 下确认条件的日期。［IAS 21 第 22 段］。即期汇率指立即交付的汇率。［IAS 21 第 8 段］。对于收入、费用、利得和损失而言，使用那些要素被确认当日的即期汇率。通常情况下，将数量众多的收入、费用、利得和损失按其各自确认日的实际汇率进行折算是不切实可行的；因此，管理层可能使用与实际汇率近似的汇率，例如平均汇率。

7.51 上述的那些要求似乎是直接的，但其应用可能会产生一些问题。其中包括：交易日的确定，有时交易日并非是显而易见的；确定一个平均汇率来作为实际汇率的近似汇率；以及在一个以上汇率有效的情况下，选择适当的汇率进行外币交易折算。

平均汇率的确定

7.52 管理层可能使用某一期间的平均汇率来替代每一交易发生日的实际汇率记录外币交易，只要该期间内未发生重大变动。涉及少量外币交易的主体一般不太可能使用平均汇率。折算大额、一次性的交易也不太可能使用平均汇率，而应该是以实际汇率进行记录。IAS 21 允许的弹性做法很可能最有益于那些涉及大量不同货币交易的主体或者那些维持多币种分类账的主体。然而，准则中未提供如何确定此类汇率的指引。

ⓒ 2013 普华永道（PricewaterhouseCoopers）版权所有。

transactions in different currencies, or that maintain multi-currency ledgers. However, no guidance is provided in the standard as to how such a rate is determined.

7.53 Determining an average rate and its use in practice depends on a number of factors, such as: the frequency and value of transactions undertaken; the period over which the rate will apply; the extent of any seasonal trade variation and the desirability of using a weighting procedure as well as the acceptable level of materiality and the nature of the entity's accounting systems. There are a large number of methods under which an average rate can be calculated. These range from simple monthly or quarterly averages to more sophisticated methods using appropriate weighting that reflects changes both in exchange rates and in the volume of business. The choice of the period to be used for calculating the average rate will depend on the extent to which daily exchange rates fluctuate in the period selected. If exchange rates are relatively stable over a period of one month for example, the average exchange rate for that month can be used as an approximation to the daily rate. If, however, there is volatility of exchange rates, it may be appropriate to calculate an average rate for a shorter period such as a week. Whatever period is chosen, materiality is likely to be an important consideration.

7.54 An entity may use an actual average rate or an estimated average rate, depending on the circumstances. An actual average rate is likely to be used where there is some delay between the date when the transactions occurred and the date when they are recorded. In other situations, it may be necessary for an entity to use an estimated average rate for a period rather than wait for the period to end in order to calculate an actual average rate. This estimate may be based on the average of daily exchange rates for the previous period or the closing rate of the previous period. Whichever basis is used, it will be necessary to ensure than the estimated average rate is a close approximation of the actual rates prevailing during the period. If it is not, the rate should be revised accordingly.

Multiple exchange rates

7.55 Some countries may operate more than one exchange rate. When several

© 2013 PricewaterhouseCoopers LLP. All rights reserved.

7.53 平均汇率的确定及其在实务中的使用取决于多种因素，诸如：所从事的交易的频率及价值；汇率的适用期间；季节性交易的变化范围；使用加权方法是否可取和可接受的重要性水平以及主体会计系统的性质。计算平均汇率有许多种方法，从简单的月度或季度平均法，到以采用同时能够反映汇率及业务量变动的适当权重的比较复杂的方法。选择用于计算平均汇率的期间是取决于所选期间内每日汇率的波动幅度。例如，如果汇率在一个月的期间内相对稳定，该月的平均汇率可以作为每日汇率的近似汇率。然而，如果汇率波动较大，计算更短期间（诸如一周）的平均汇率可能更为适当。无论选择哪一期间，重要性都很可能是一个重要的考虑因素。

7.54 一个主体可能视情况使用实际平均汇率或估计平均汇率。在交易发生日与交易记录日有一定延迟的情况下，很可能使用实际平均汇率。在其他情形下，主体可能需要使用某一期间的估计平均汇率，而不是等到期末再计算实际平均汇率。此估计可能基于之前期间的日平均汇率或期末汇率。无论使用哪种基础，将需要确保估计的平均汇率是该期间实际汇率的近似汇率；如果不是，则应当对该汇率进行相应的修正。

多元汇率

7.55 某些国家可能同时运作多个汇率。当存在多个可供使用的汇率时，用

ⓒ 2013 普华永道（PricewaterhouseCoopers）版权所有。

exchange rates are available, the rate used to translate and record the foreign currency transactions and balances is that at which the future cash flows represented by the transaction or balance could have been settled if those cash flows had occurred at the measurement date. [IAS 21 para 26]. Chapter 31 contains an example of an entity disclosing the exchange rate it used when several are available (Table 31.2.1). When translating a net investment under IAS 21, the rate used would often be the dividend remittance rate, but another rate may be more appropriate if the proceeds would in practice be remitted in another way. Where a country has multiple exchange rates, judgement is often required to determine which exchange rate qualifies as a spot rate that can be used for translation under IAS 21. In determining whether a rate is a spot rate, an entity should consider whether currency is obtainable at a quoted rate and whether the quoted rate is available for immediate delivery. In practice, a normal administrative delay in obtaining funds would be acceptable.

Suspension of rates

7.56 Countries may experience economic conditions from time to time that affect the free-market convertibility of the local currency. As a result, the exchangeability between two currencies may be temporarily unavailable at the transaction date or a subsequent balance sheet date. IAS 21 requires entities to use the rate on the first subsequent date at which exchanges could be made. [IAS 21 para 26].

7.57 Doubts as to convertibility may arise if, for example, a Canadian entity makes a long-term currency loan to an overseas supplier but restrictions on the remittance of funds are imposed by the overseas country sometime before the balance sheet date. Such restrictions may arise as a result of currency devaluation, political upheaval or severe exchange control regulations in the overseas country. Management should use the rate on the first subsequent date at which exchanges could be made following restoration of normal conditions.

Example – Suspension of foreign exchange rates

In October 20X3, entity A, which is incorporated in the UK, used surplus

© 2013 PricewaterhouseCoopers LLP. All rights reserved.

以折算和记录该外币交易或余额的汇率是假如交易或余额所代表的现金流量在计量日即已发生，可以用来结算该现金流量的汇率。[IAS 21 第 26 段]。第三十一章包含了一个主体披露其在有多个汇率可供使用时所采用的汇率（表 31. 2. 1）。当按照 IAS 21 折算净投资时，使用的汇率应该是经常股利汇款时的汇率，但如果实务中该款项应该是以其他方式汇出的，那么另一个汇率可能是更适当的。在一个国家拥有多元汇率的情况下，通常需要运用判断以决定哪一个汇率是符合 IAS 21 要求的可以用于折算的即期汇率。在决定一个汇率是否是即期汇率时，主体应当考虑该货币是否能够按报价汇率取得以及该报价汇率是否可用于立即交付。实务中，作业上的正常延迟是可以接受的。

折算汇率的暂停使用

7. 56　各个国家可能会不时地经历各种影响当地货币在自由市场的可兑换性的经济状况。由此导致两种货币间在交易日或之后的资产负债表日可能暂时不可兑换。IAS 21 要求主体使用期后两种货币可以兑换时的首日汇率。[IAS 21 第 26 段]。

7. 57　可能会对于可兑换性产生疑问。例如，某一加拿大主体贷给某一海外供应商一笔长期贷款，而该海外国家在资产负债表日前对资金汇出加以限制。此类限制可能由该海外国家的货币贬值、政治动乱或严厉的外汇管制而引起。管理层应当使用恢复正常状况后的首日汇率。

示例——外币折算汇率的暂停

于 20X3 年 10 月，设立于英国的主体 A 使用多余的外币向其海外供应商

ⓒ 2013 普华永道（PricewaterhouseCoopers）版权所有。

currency to make a long-term loan of FC 15m to its overseas supplier. The loan was made when the exchange rate was £1 = FC 5.00 and is repayable on 30 September 20X5, entity A's year-end. Initially, the loan is translated and recorded in entity A's books at £3m. The amount that entity A ultimately receives depends on the rate of exchange ruling on the date when the loan is repaid.

On 28 September 20X5, a few days before the due date of the loan's repayment, the exchange rate was £1 = FC 6. On the same date the local government announced that a devaluation would occur on 2 October 20X5 and all foreign exchange transactions would be suspended until 3 October 20X5. On 2 October 20X5, foreign exchange transactions were executed but left unsettled until the following day when a new rate was established. On 3 October 20X5 a new rate of £1 = FC 7.5 was established and was effective for transactions left unsettled the previous day.

An official exchange rate at 30 September 20X5 is temporarily unavailable. In this situation, the exchange rate was temporarily lacking and the rate established on 3 October 20X5, the first subsequent date, is the appropriate rate to use for translating the monetary asset at the balance sheet date of 30 September 20X5. Therefore, entity A would record the loan receivable at £2m and recognise a foreign exchange loss of £1m in profit or loss.

Subsequent measurement

7.58 A foreign currency transaction may give rise to assets and liabilities that are denominated in a foreign currency. The procedure for translating such assets and liabilities into the entity's functional currency at each balance sheet date will depend on whether they are monetary or non-monetary.

Translation of monetary items

7.59 Monetary items are units of currency held and assets and liabilities to be received or paid in fixed or determinable number of units of currency. [IAS 21 para 8]. The essential feature of a monetary item is a right to receive (or an

© 2013 PricewaterhouseCoopers LLP. All rights reserved.

提供长期贷款 FC 1,500 万元。贷款发生日的汇率为 1 英镑 = FC 5.00，于 20X5 年 9 月 30 日（亦即主体 A 的会计年度期末）到期偿还。在最初的时候，该贷款在主体 A 的账簿中是折算为 300 万英镑并以此记录。主体 A 最终收到的金额取决于该贷款偿还当日的汇率。

于 20X5 年 9 月 28 日，即贷款到期偿还日的几天前，汇率为 1 英镑 = FC 6.00。就在同一天，当地政府宣布该国货币将于 20X5 年 10 月 2 日贬值，所有外币交易将暂停，直到 20X5 年 10 月 3 日。于 20X5 年 10 月 2 日，执行的外币交易将于次日新汇率确定后再进行结算。于 20X5 年 10 月 3 日，新汇率确定为 1 英镑 = FC 7.5，该汇率对那些在前一日未结算的交易有效。

20X5 年 9 月 30 日的官方汇率暂时无法获得。在这种情形下，汇率暂时无法取得而 20X5 年 10 月 3 日为汇率确定后的首日，该日汇率是用来折算 20X5 年 9 月 30 日资产负债表中的货币性资产的适当汇率。因此，主体 A 应该会记录应收贷款 200 万英镑，并将 100 万英镑的汇兑损失确认为损益。

后续计量

7.58 外币交易可能会产生以外币计价的资产和负债。在每一个资产负债表日，将这些资产和负债折算成主体功能货币的程序取决于其是货币性项目，还是非货币性项目。

货币性项目的折算

7.59 货币性项目是指持有的货币单位和将以固定或可确定数量的货币单位收取的资产或者偿付的负债。[IAS 21 第 8 段]。货币性项目的基本特征是有权收取（或有义务交付）固定或可确定金额的货币单位。例如：

ⓒ 2013 普华永道（PricewaterhouseCoopers）版权所有。

obligation to deliver) a fixed or determinable number of units of currency. Examples are

- Financial assets such as cash, bank balances and receivables.
- Financial liabilities such as debt.
- Provisions that are settled in cash.
- Pensions and other employee benefits to be paid in cash, deferred taxes and cash dividends that are recognised as a liability.
- Derivative financial instruments, such as forward exchange contracts, foreign currency swaps and options are also monetary items as they are settled at a future date.

Short-term monetary items are those that fall due within one year of the balance sheet date; long-term monetary items are those that fall due more than one year after the balance sheet date.

7.60 In some instances, it may not be readily apparent whether an item should be regarded as a monetary or a non-monetary item. Management should consider whether the item represents an amount to be received or paid in money, in which case it would fall to be treated as a monetary item.

7.61 For an item to qualify as a monetary item, it does not need to be recovered or settled in cash. A contract to receive (or deliver) a variable number of an entity's own equity instruments or a variable amount of assets in which the fair value to be received (or delivered) equals a fixed or determinable number of units of currency is also a monetary item. [IAS 21 para 16]. In other words, an entity's own equity instruments can be used 'as currency' in a contract that can be settled at a value equal to a fixed or a determinable amount. Such a contract is not an equity instrument, but a monetary financial asset or a liability. Not all financial assets should be treated as monetary items. For example, an investment in an equity instrument is not a monetary item – there is no right to receive a fixed or determinable amount of cash. [IAS 39 para AG83].

7.62 IAS 21 requires entities to translate foreign currency monetary items outstanding at the end of balance sheet date using the closing rate. [IAS 21 para

© 2013 PricewaterhouseCoopers LLP. All rights reserved.

- 金融资产，诸如现金、银行存款和应收款项。
- 金融负债，诸如债务。
- 以现金结算的预计负债。
- 以现金支付的养老金和其他职工福利、递延所得税和确认为负债的现金股利。
- 衍生金融工具，诸如远期外汇合同、外汇互换和期权等也属于货币性项目，因为其会在将来的某一天结算。

短期货币性项目是指于资产负债表日后一年内到期的项目；长期货币性项目是指资产负债表日后一年以上到期的项目。

7.60 在某些情况下，一个项目应当视为货币性项目还是非货币性项目，可能不是显而易见的。管理层应当考虑该项目是否代表着将收取或偿付一定金额的货币，如果是，则该项目应该是视作货币性项目的。

7.61 作为货币性项目，其并不是必须以现金收回或结算的。一份收取（或交付）可变数量的主体自身权益工具或可变金额的资产的合同，如果合同中所要收取（或交付）的公允价值等于一个固定或可确定数量的货币单位，则也是属于货币性项目。[IAS 21 第 16 段]。换言之，在一份可以按照等同于某一固定或可确定金额的价值进行结算的合同中，主体自身的权益工具可以“作为货币”使用。这样的合同不是权益工具，而是一项货币性金融资产或负债。并不是所有的金融资产都应当被视为货币性项目，例如对权益工具的投资不是货币性项目，因为没有收取固定或可确定金额的现金的权利。[IAS 39 AG 第 83 段]。

7.62 IAS 21 要求主体使用期末汇率折算其在资产负债表日持有的外币货币性项目。[IAS 21 第 23（a）段]。期末汇率指资产负债表日的即期汇率。

© 2013 普华永道（PricewaterhouseCoopers）版权所有。

23(a)]. The closing rate is the spot exchange rate at the balance sheet date. [IAS 21 para 8]. A rate of exchange that is fixed under the terms of the relevant contract cannot be used to translate monetary assets and liabilities. Translating a monetary item at the contracted rate under the terms of a relevant contract is a form of hedge accounting that is not permitted under IAS 39. The treatment of the exchange differences that arise on translating a monetary item at the balance sheet date is considered from paragraphs 7.67 below.

Translation of non-monetary items

7.63 Non-monetary items are all items other than monetary items. In other words, the right to receive (or an obligation to deliver) a fixed or determinable number of units of currency is absent in a non-monetary item. Typical examples are:

- Intangible assets.
- Goodwill.
- Property, plant and equipment.
- Inventories.
- Amounts pre-paid for goods and services (pre-paid rent).
- Equity investments.
- Provisions that are to be settled by the delivery of a non-monetary asset.

[IAS 21 para 16].

7.63.1 Advances paid and received (including pre-payments) can be difficult to classify as monetary or non-monetary. An example of a non-monetary item is an advance payment for goods that, absent a default by the counterparty, must be settled by the counterparty delivering the goods. However, if an advance is refundable in circumstances other than a default by either party, this may indicate that it is a monetary item as the item is receivable in units of currency.

7.64 Translation of non-monetary items depends on whether they are recognised

© 2013 PricewaterhouseCoopers LLP. All rights reserved.

[IAS 21 第 8 段]。相关合同条款中所固定的汇率不能用于折算货币性资产和负债。以相关合同条款中规定的汇率折算货币性项目是 IAS 39 所不允许的一种套期会计形式。因折算资产负债表日的货币性项目而产生的汇兑差额的处理方法在下文自第 7.67 段起进行讨论。

非货币性项目的折算

7.63　非货币性项目是指除货币性项目以外的项目；换言之，非货币性项目不具有收取（或支付）固定或可确定数量的货币单位的权利（或义务）。典型的例子有：

- 无形资产。
- 商誉。
- 不动产、工厂和设备。
- 存货。
- 为取得商品和劳务的预付金额（预付租金）。
- 股权投资。
- 以交付非货币性资产进行结算的预计负债。

[IAS 21 第 16 段]。

7.63.1　预付和预收款项（包括提前支付的款项）可能难以区分是货币性的，还是非货币性的。非货币性项目的一个例子是在交易对方没有违约的情况下，必须以交付货物进行结算的预付货款。然而，如果在交易双方都没有违约的情形下，一项预付款是可以返还的，这可能表明其是一项货币性项目，因为该项目是以一定数量的货币单位收取的。

7.64　非货币性项目的折算取决于其是以历史成本，还是以公允价值进行确

© 2013 普华永道（PricewaterhouseCoopers）版权所有。

at historical cost or at fair value. For example, property, plant and equipment may be measured in terms of historical cost or revalued amounts in accordance with IAS 16.

7.65 Non-monetary items that are measured in terms of historical cost in a foreign currency are translated using the exchange rate at the date of the transaction. [IAS 21 para 23(b)]. This means that such assets are recorded at historical cost, and no retranslation of the asset is required at subsequent balance sheet dates. However, if the asset is impaired, the recoverable amount is translated at the exchange rate ruling at the date when that value was determined (for example, the closing rate at the balance sheet date). Comparing the previously recorded historical cost with the recoverable amount may or may not result in recognising an impairment loss in the functional currency. For example, an entity's functional currency is sterling. A foreign currency asset costing FC 925,000 is recorded at the date of purchase at £500,000 when £1 = FC 1.85. At a subsequent balance sheet date, the asset's recoverable amount in foreign currency is FC 787,500 when £1 = FC 1.5. Although there is impairment loss in foreign currency, no impairment loss is recognised, because the recoverable amount at the balance sheet date of £525,000 is higher than the carrying value.

7.66 Non-monetary assets that are measured at fair value in a foreign currency are translated using the exchange rates at the date when the fair value was determined. [IAS 21 para 23(c)]. For example, a UK entity has a euro-denominated investment property located in France that is carried at fair value with gains and losses from changes in fair value recognised in profit or loss for the period in which they arise, in accordance with IAS 40. The fair values measured initially in euros due to the property's appreciation in value are translated to sterling at the exchange rate ruling at the relevant measurement dates. The resulting change in fair value in sterling includes foreign exchange differences arising on the retranslation of the opening euro carrying value. This exchange difference is recognised as part of the change in fair value in profit or loss for the period.

© 2013 PricewaterhouseCoopers LLP. All rights reserved.

认的。例如，根据 IAS 16，不动产、工厂和设备可能以历史成本或重估金额进行计量。

7.65　以历史成本计量的外币非货币性项目按交易日的汇率折算。[IAS 21 第 23（b）段]。这意味着此类资产以历史成本记录，且在资产负债表日后无须重新折算。然而，如果此类资产发生减值，可收回金额按照该价值确定日的汇率折算（例如，资产负债表日的期末汇率）。将之前记录的历史成本与可收回金额相比较，不一定会导致确认以功能货币计价的减值损失。例如，某一主体的功能货币为英镑，其一项成本为 FC 925,000 的外币资产在购买日以 500,000 英镑入账（购买当日汇率为 1 英镑 = FC 1.85）。在资产负债表日后的某天，该资产的外币可收回金额为 FC 787,500（当日汇率为 1 英镑 = FC 1.5）。尽管以外币来看是有减值损失，但由于在资产负债表日的可收回金额 525,000 英镑大于该资产的账面价值，因此减值损失无需确认。

7.66　以公允价值计量的外币非货币性资产按其公允价值确定日的汇率折算。[IAS 21 第 23（c）段]。例如，某一英国主体有一处位于法国并以欧元计价的投资性房地产，按照 IAS 40 以公允价值载于账上，公允价值变动产生的利得或损失计入当期损益。由于该房地产增值，初始以欧元计量的公允价值按照相关计量日的汇率折算为英镑。由此导致的以英镑表示的公允价值变动包含了重新折算期初欧元账面价值而产生的汇兑差额。这一汇兑差额作为公允价值变动的一部分计入当期损益。

© 2013 普华永道（PricewaterhouseCoopers）版权所有。

Recognition of exchange differences

Monetary items

7. 67 Exchange differences arising on the settlement of monetary items, or on translating monetary items at rates different from those at which they were translated on initial recognition during the period or in previous financial statements, are recognised in profit or loss in the period in which they arise, except as described in paragraph 7. 70 below. [IAS 21 para 28].

7. 68 When monetary items arise from a foreign currency transaction and there is a change in exchange rate between the transaction date and the date of settlement, an exchange difference results. Where a transaction is *settled* within the same accounting period at an exchange rate that differs from the rate used when the transaction was initially recorded, the exchange difference is recognised in the income statement of the period in which the settlement takes place. [IAS 21 para 29]. It is appropriate to recognise such exchange differences as part of the profit or loss for that year, as the exchange difference will have been reflected in the cash flow at the time of the settlement.

Example – Treatment of a foreign currency denominated purchase of plant

In March 20X5, a UK entity purchases plant for use in the UK from an overseas entity for FC 1,980, 000. At the date the entity purchases the plant, the exchange rate is £1 = FC 1. 65. The purchase price is to be settled in three months, although delivery is made immediately. The UK entity records both the plant and the monetary liability at £1,200, 000 (FC 1,980, 000/£1. 65). The entity will not need to translate the plant again. At the settlement date, the exchange rate is £1 = FC 1. 75. The actual amount the UK entity will pay to settle the liability is therefore £1, 131, 429. The entity should include the gain on exchange of £68, 751 (that is, £1, 200, 000 - £1, 131, 429) in arriving at its profit or loss.

7. 69 Where a monetary item arising from a foreign currency transaction remains

© 2013 PricewaterhouseCoopers LLP. All rights reserved.

汇兑差额的确认

货币性项目

7.67　除下文第7.70段所述的情形外，货币性项目的结算或以不同于当期或前期财务报表中初始确认时进行折算的汇率对货币性项目进行折算所产生的汇兑差额，在其产生当期确认于损益。[IAS 21 第28段]。

7.68　当交易日与结算日之间汇率发生变动时，由外币交易形成的货币性项目将产生汇兑差额。在一项交易是在同一个会计期间内、以不同于该交易初始记录时所采用的汇率进行结算的情况下，该汇兑差额应于结算发生当期确认于利润表中。[IAS 21 第29段]。由于该汇兑差额将会于结算时点在现金流中反映出来，因此将其确认为当年损益的一部分是适当的。

示例——以外币计价的购买工厂的会计处理

某一英国主体于20X5年3月，以FC 1,980,000向一境外主体购买工厂设备以供其在英国使用。该主体购买工厂当日的汇率为1英镑 = FC1.65。尽管该工厂是立即交付的，但是购买价款将于三个月内结算。该英国主体将该工厂和货币性负债同时记录为1,200,000英镑（FC 1,980,000/1.65英镑）。该主体不需要再次折算该工厂。于结算日，汇率为1英镑 = FC 1.75。因此，该英国主体将实际支付1,131,429英镑以结算负债。该主体应当将产生的汇兑收益68,751英镑（即1,200,000英镑 - 1,131,429英镑）计入其当期损益。

7.69　在外币交易产生的货币性项目于资产负债表日仍未结算的情况下，以

ⓒ 2013 普华永道（PricewaterhouseCoopers）版权所有。

outstanding at the balance sheet date, an exchange difference arises as a consequence of recording the foreign currency transaction at the rate ruling at the date of the transaction (or when it was translated at a previous balance sheet date) and the subsequent retranslation of the monetary item to the rate ruling at the balance sheet date. Such exchange differences are reported as part of the profit or loss for the year.

7.69.1 Monetary assets classified as available-for-sale in accordance with IAS 39 are carried at fair value but are treated for the purpose of calculating foreign exchange differences as if they were carried at amortised cost. The exchange differences resulting from changes in amortised cost are recognised in the income statement. [IAS 39 AG 83]. Other fair value gains and losses on available-for-sale monetary financial assets are required to be recognised in other comprehensive income. [IAS 39 para 55(b), IG E 3.2]. See chapter 9 of IFRS Manual of Accounting – Financial Instruments for an example of the treatment of foreign exchange gains and losses on monetary available-for-sale assets.

7.70 Not all exchange differences on monetary items are reported in the income statement. There are number of exceptions. These are:

- A monetary item that is designated as a hedging instrument in a cash flow hedge. Any exchange difference that forms part of the gain or loss on the hedging instrument is recognised in other comprehensive income. [IAS 39 para 95].

- A monetary item that is designated as a hedge of a net investment *in consolidated financial statements.* The exchange difference on the hedging instrument that is considered to be an effective hedge is recognised in other comprehensive income. [IAS 39 para 102]. See from paragraph 7.108 onwards below.

- A monetary item that forms part of the net investment in a foreign operation in the consolidated financial statements. See from paragraph 7.93 onwards below.

Non-monetary items

7.71 When a gain or loss on a non-monetary item is recognised directly in other

© 2013 PricewaterhouseCoopers LLP. All rights reserved.

交易日汇率记录该外币交易（或该交易在前期资产负债表日进行折算）与随后以资产负债表日的汇率重新折算将会产生汇兑差额。此类汇兑差额作为当年损益的一部分进行列报。

7.69.1 根据IAS 39，分类为可供出售的货币性资产应以公允价值载于账上，但在计算汇兑差额时视同为其以摊余成本载于账上。摊余成本变动所导致的汇兑差额确认于利润表中。[IAS 39 实施指南第83 段]。可供出售的货币性金融资产的其他公允价值利得或损失必须计入其他综合收益。［IAS 39 第55（b）段，IG 第E.3.2 段］。参见《国际财务报告准则实务指引——金融工具系列》第九章中的一个关于可供出售的货币性资产汇兑损益会计处理的示例。

7.70 并非所有货币性项目产生的汇兑差额均在利润表中列报，而是存在很多例外情况。它们是：

- 在现金流量套期中被指定为套期工具的货币性项目。任何构成套期工具利得或损失组成部分的任何汇兑差额均计入其他综合收益。［IAS 39 第95段］。

- *在合并财务报表中*被指定为净投资套期的货币性项目。被认为是有效套期的套期工具所产生的汇兑差额应计入其他综合收益。［IAS 39 第102 段］。参见第7.108 段及其下文。

- 合并财务报表中构成境外经营净投资组成部分的货币性项目。参见第7.93段及其下文。

非货币性项目

7.71 当某一非货币性项目产生的利得或损失直接计入其他综合收益时，该

ⓒ 2013 普华永道（PricewaterhouseCoopers）版权所有。

comprehensive income, any exchange component of that gain or loss is recognised directly in other comprehensive income. [IAS 39 para 30]. For example, an entity purchases equity securities denominated in a foreign currency that are classified as available for sale. Under IAS 39, the equity securities are carried at fair value. Any changes in fair value that are recognised directly in other comprehensive income also include any related foreign exchange element. [IAS 39 paras 55 (b), AG83]. Another example is where a property denominated in a foreign currency is revalued. Any exchange difference arising when the property is translated at the rate of exchange ruling at the valuation date is reported directly in other comprehensive income along with other changes in value.

Example – Translation of a revalued foreign asset

A UK entity with a sterling functional currency has a property located in the US, which it acquired at a cost of US $ 1. 8 m when the exchange rate was £ 1 = US $ 1. 6. The property was revalued to US $ 2. 16m at the balance sheet date. The exchange rate at the balance sheet date was £ 1 = US $ 1. 8.

Ignoring depreciation, the amount that would be reported directly to equity is:

	£
Value at balance sheet date = US $ 2,160, 000 @ 1. 8 =	1, 200, 000
Value at acquisition date = US $ 1,800, 000 @ 1. 6 =	1, 125, 000
Revaluation surplus recognised in other comprehensive income	75, 000

The revaluation surplus may be analysed as follows:

Change in fair value = US $ 360, 000 @ 1. 8 =	200, 000
Exchange component of change = US $ 1,800, 000 @ 1. 8 – US $ 1,800, 000 @ 1. 6	(125, 000)
Revaluation surplus recognised in other comprehensive income	75, 000

7. 72 On the other hand, when a gain or loss on a non-monetary item is recognised in profit or loss, any exchange component of that gain or loss is also recognised in profit or loss. [IAS 21 para 38].

© 2013 PricewaterhouseCoopers LLP. All rights reserved.

项利得或损失的任何汇兑部分均直接计入其他综合收益。[IAS 39 第 30 段]。例如，某一主体购买以外币计价的、分类为可供出售的权益证券。根据 IAS 39，该权益证券以公允价值载于账上。任何直接确认于其他综合收益中的公允价值变动也包括任何相关的外币汇兑因素。[IAS 39 第 55（b）段，实施指南第 83 段]。另一个例子是在以外币计价的不动产被重估的情况下，该不动产以估值日的汇率进行折算，由此产生的汇兑差额应与其他价值变动一起直接报告于其他综合收益。

示例——重估后的境外资产的折算

某一功能货币为英镑的英国主体有一处位于美国的不动产，购买成本为 1, 800, 000 美元，当时的汇率为 1 英镑 = 1. 6 美元。该不动产于资产负债表日重估为 2, 160, 000 美元。资产负债表日的汇率为 1 英镑 = 1. 8 美元。

不考虑折旧，直接报告于权益的金额应该为：

	英镑
资产负债表日价值 = 2,160, 000 美元按汇率 1. 8 折算 =	1, 200, 000
购买日价值 = 1 ,800,000 美元按汇率 1. 6 折算 =	1, 125, 000
确认于其他综合收益的重估增值	75, 000
重估增值的分析如下：	
公允价值变动 = 360, 000 美元按汇率 1. 8 折算 =	200, 000
汇率变动部分 = 1 ,800,000 美元按汇率 1. 8 折算 − 1 ,800,000 美元按汇率 1. 6 折算	(125, 000)
确认于其他综合收益的重估增值	75, 000

7. 72　另一方面，当某一非货币性项目产生的利得和损失确认于损益时，该利得或损失的汇兑部分也应直接确认于损益。[IAS 21 第 38 段]。

© 2013 普华永道（PricewaterhouseCoopers）版权所有。

Example – Translation of an impaired foreign asset

A UK entity with a sterling functional currency has a property located in the US, which was acquired at a cost of US $ 1. 8m when the exchange rate was £1 = US $ 1. 6. The property is carried at cost. At the balance sheet date the recoverable amount of the property as a result of an impairment review amounted to US $ 1. 62m. The exchange rate at the balance sheet date was £1 = US $ 1. 8.

Ignoring depreciation, the impairment loss that would be reported in the income statement as a result of the impairment is:

	£
Carrying value at balance sheet date – US $ 1,620, 000 @ 1. 8 =	900, 000
Historical cost – US $ 1,800, 000 @ 1. 6 =	1, 125, 000
Impairment loss recognised in profit or loss	(225, 000)
The impairment loss may be analysed as follows:	
Change in value due to impairment = US $ 180, 000 @ 1. 8 =	(100, 000)
Exchange component of change = US $ 1,800,000 @ 1. 8 – US $ 1,800,000 @ 1. 6	(125, 000)
Impairment loss recognised in profit or loss	(225, 000)

Foreign currency translation of financial statements

Introduction

7. 73 Accounting for transactions in foreign currencies that are directly undertaken by an entity and that are measured and expressed in the entity's functional currency is addressed earlier in this chapter. Where foreign activities are undertaken through foreign operations, the financial statements of those foreign operations are translated so that they can be included in the reporting entity's financial statements

© 2013 PricewaterhouseCoopers LLP. All rights reserved.

示例——发生减值的境外资产的折算

某一功能货币为英镑的英国主体有一处位于美国的不动产，购买成本为1,800,000美元，当时的汇率为1英镑=1.6美元。该不动产以成本载于账上。减值复核表明该不动产于资产负债表日的可收回金额为1,620,000美元。资产负债表日的汇率为1英镑=1.8美元。

不考虑折旧，由于导致的列示于利润表中的减值损失应该为：

	英镑
资产负债表日账面价值－1,620,000美元按汇率1.8折算＝	900,000
历史成本－1,800,000美元按汇率1.6折算＝	1,125,000
确认于损益的减值损失	(225,000)
减值损失的分析如下：	
因减值产生的价值变动＝180,000美元按汇率1.8折算＝	(100,000)
汇率变动部分＝1,800,000美元按汇率1.8折算－1,800,000美元按汇率1.6折算	(125,000)
确认于损益的减值损失	(225,000)

财务报表的外币换算

引言

7.73　主体直接进行的，并以主体功能货币计量和表示的外币交易的会计处理已在本章上文阐述。在境外活动是通过境外经营进行的情况下，那些境外经营的财务报表将被折算，以便可以通过合并，比例合并或权益法将其包括在报告主体的财务报表中。折算过程阐述了用以折算境外经营利润表和资产负债表的适当汇率以及汇率变动的财务影响如何确认于报告主体的财务报

ⓒ 2013 普华永道（PricewaterhouseCoopers）版权所有。

by consolidation, proportional consolidation or the equity method. The process of translation addresses the appropriate exchange rates to use for translating the income statement and the balance sheet of the foreign operation and how the financial effects of changes in exchange rates are recognised in the reporting entity's financial statements.

7.74 The standard permits an entity to present its financial statements in a currency other than its functional currency. The currency in which the financial statements are presented is referred to as the 'presentation currency'. [IAS 21 para 8]. There is no requirement in the standard for an entity to present its financial statements in its functional currency, which most faithfully portrays the economic effect of transactions and events on the entity. The IASB explains why entities are permitted to present their financial statements in any currency in paragraphs BC10 to BC14 of the Basis for Conclusions of IAS 21.

7.75 Although entities have a free choice in the selection of the presentation currency, they are likely to use the functional currency, the currency used for measurement, as the presentation currency. If management uses an alternative currency, disclosure of the reasons for selecting a different currency is required. There must, therefore, be substantive and valid reasons for choosing an alternative presentation currency. For example, in some countries, an entity may be required by local and legal regulations to present its financial statements in the local currency even if this is not its functional currency.

Translation to the presentation currency

7.76 Selecting a presentation currency that is different from the functional currency requires a translation from the functional currency into the presentation currency. For example, when a group contains individual entities with different functional currencies, the results and financial position of each entity is expressed in a common currency so that consolidated financial statements may be presented. IAS 21 has prescribed a translation methodology for translating from the functional currency to a different presentation currency. This translation methodology seeks to ensure that the financial and operational relationships between underlying amounts established in the entity's primary economic environment and measured in its

© 2013 PricewaterhouseCoopers LLP. All rights reserved.

表中。

7.74　准则允许实主体以非功能货币列报其财务报表。财务报表列报的货币称为“列报货币”。[IAS 21 第 8 段]。准则中没有要求主体必须以其功能货币（即最真实描绘主体交易和事项的经济影响的货币）列报其财务报表。IASB 在 IAS 21 的结论基础第 10 段至第 14 段中解释了为什么允许主体以任何货币列报其财务报表。

7.75　尽管主体可以自由选择功能货币，其可能仍会使用功能货币（计量所使用的货币）作为列报货币。如果管理层使用另一种货币，要求披露选择另一种货币的理由。因此，选择另一种列报货币必须有实质的与真实的理由。例如，在某些国家，当地法规可能要求主体以当地货币列报其财务报表，即使该货币不是其功能货币。

列报货币的折算

7.76　选择不同于功能货币的列报货币，要求主体将功能货币折算为列报货币。例如，当某个集团包含使用不同功能货币的多个个别主体时，每一个主体的经营成果和财务状况应以一种共同的货币表示，从而可能可以列报合并财务报表。IAS 21 已经规定了将功能货币折算为不同的列报货币的折算方法。这一方法力求确保在折算为不同的计量货币时，保留在主体主要经济环境中建立的、以其功能货币计量的相关金额之间财务和经营关系。该方法在下一段中进行描述。另一种折算方法适用于以恶性通货膨胀经济中的货币为功能货币的主体。这一方法在第三十一章中进行描述。

ⓒ 2013 普华永道（PricewaterhouseCoopers）版权所有。

functional currency are preserved when translated into a different measurement currency. The translation method is described in the next paragraph. A different translation methodology applies to an entity whose functional currency is the currency of a hyper-inflationary economy. This method is described in chapter 31.

7.77 The translation methodology referred to above requires an entity's results and financial position whose functional currency is not the currency of a hyper-inflationary economy to be translated into a different presentation currency using the following procedures:

- Assets and liabilities for each balance sheet presented (including comparatives) are translated at the closing rate at the date of that balance sheet.

  Use of a constant rate of exchange for all items on the balance sheet maintains the relationship in the retranslated financial statements as existed in the foreign operation's financial statements. Therefore, for example, fixed assets are the same proportion of long-term liabilities.

- Income and expenses for each income statement (including comparatives) is translated at exchange rates at the dates of the transactions. For practical reasons, a rate that approximates the exchange rates at the dates of the transactions – for example, an average rate for the period – is often used to translate income and expense items. However, if exchange rates fluctuate significantly, the use of the average rate for a period is inappropriate (see para 7.81 below).

  The use of a closing rate is more likely to preserve the financial results and relationships that existed prior to translation, but the use of an actual or average rate reflects more fairly the profits or losses and cash flows as they accrue to the group throughout the period.

- All resulting exchange differences are recognised in other comprehensive income and accumulated as a separate component of equity.

[IAS 21 paras 39, 40].

Equity items

7.77.1 The standard is silent on how to translate items that are recognised

© 2013 PricewaterhouseCoopers LLP. All rights reserved.

7.77 上文提及的折算方法要求主体（其功能货币不是恶性通货膨胀经济下的货币）的经营成果和财务状况按照下列程序折算为不同的列报货币：

■ 每一资产负债表列报的资产和负债（包括比较数据）以那一资产负债表日的期末汇率进行折算。

对资产负债表中的所有项目采用相同汇率，使得存在于境外经营财务报表中的数据关系在重新折算的财务报表中保持不变。因此，如固定资产占长期负债的比例是一致的。

■ 每一利润表中的收益和费用（包括比较数据）以交易日的汇率进行折算。出于实务理由，通常使用近似于交易日汇率的汇率（例如，当期平均汇率）以折算收益和费用项目。然而，如果汇率波动重大，使用某一期间的平均汇率是不适当的（参见下文第 7.81 段）。

使用期末汇率更可能保留折算前就存在的财务结果和关系，但是使用实际汇率或平均汇率能更真实地反映损益和现金流，因为其是集团在整个期间内累计发生的。

■ 由此产生的所有汇兑差额确认于其他综合收益，并累计为权益的一个单独组成部分。

[IAS 21 第 39、40 段]。

权益项目

7.77.1 准则没有提及如何折算直接确认于权益的项目，即尚未确认于业绩

© 2013 普华永道（PricewaterhouseCoopers）版权所有。

directly in equity, that is, items that have not been recognised through the performance statements. These will generally be recognised as a result of a transaction with a shareholder, such as share capital, share premium or treasury shares. Management has a choice of using either the historical rate or the closing rate for these items. The chosen policy should be applied consistently. If the historical rate is used, these equity items are not retranslated and the CTA will, therefore, only include the cumulative differences between opening and closing rates on total net assets, and average to closing rates on retained earnings and other performance statement items, such as AFS or hedging reserves. If the closing rate is used, the resulting exchange differences are recognised directly in equity as part of the CTA reserve. This effectively reduces the CTA that arises on retranslating the net assets. Any exchange differences arising on translating equity items are not recognised in the performance statements. They are instead recognised directly in equity, with the result that the CTA movement in equity will not equal the CTA recognised in total comprehensive income. The policy choice has no impact on the amount of total equity. The regulatory framework in some jurisdictions may mandate one treatment.

7.78 The exchange differences referred to in the last bullet point in paragraph 7.77 above comprises:

- Differences arising from translating the income statement at exchange rates at the dates of the transactions or at average rates, and assets and liabilities at the closing rate. Such exchange differences arise on items recognised in the income statement as well as in other comprehensive income.
- Differences arising on the opening net assets' retranslation at a closing rate that differs from the previous closing rate.

[IAS 21 para 41].

CTA may also include differences on retranslation of equity items, depending on the policy choice made, as described in paragraph 7.77 above.

7.79 The above exchange differences are not recognised in the income statement. This would distort the results from trading operations shown in the functional currency financial statements. Such differences, which primarily result from a

© 2013 PricewaterhouseCoopers LLP. All rights reserved.

报表的项目。通常情况下，与股东的交易（诸如股本、股本溢价、库存股）将会导致这些权益项目的确认。管理层可选择使用历史汇率或期末汇率以折算这些项目。该选择的政策应当一致地应用。如果使用历史汇率，则不再重新折算这些权益项目；因此，CTA 将仅包括净资产总额因期初汇率和期末汇率差异产生的累计差额以及留存收益和其他业绩报表项目（诸如可供出售金融资产或套期准备）因平均汇率与期末汇率差异产生的累计差额。如果使用期末汇率，产生的汇兑差额作为 CTA 的一部分直接确认于权益。这有效地减少了净资产重新折算所产生的 CTA。折算权益项目产生的任何汇兑差额均不确认于业绩报表，而是直接确认于权益；由此导致权益中的 CTA 变动将不等于确认于其他综合收益的 CTA。某些地区的法规框架可能强制要求某一种处理方法。

7.78 上文第 7.77 段中最后一点提及的汇兑差额包括：

- 以交易日汇率或平均汇率折算利润表以及以期末汇率折算资产和负债而产生的差额。此类汇兑差额由确认于利润表及其他综合收益中的项目所产生。

- 以不同于前期期末汇率的当期期末汇率折算期初净资产所产生的差额。

[IAS 21 第 41 段]。

如上文第 7.77 段所述，根据主体所选择的政策，CTA 还可能包括权益项目重新折算所产生的汇兑差额。

7.79 上述汇兑差额不确认于利润表，否则应该会扭曲以功能货币列示的财务报表中的交易经营结果。此类主要由折算过程导致的汇兑差额是与境外经营的交易业绩或财务经营无关的，其尤其无法代表或计量实际或预期现金流

ⓒ 2013 普华永道（PricewaterhouseCoopers）版权所有。

translation process, are unrelated to the foreign operation's trading performance or financial operations; in particular, they do not represent or measure changes in actual or prospective cash flows. They do have an impact on the net investment that may be realised upon sale or liquidation, but that effect is related to the net investment and not to the investee's operations. It is, therefore, inappropriate to regard them as profits or losses. Hence, they are recognised in a separate component of other comprehensive income.

7.80 The IASB chose the translation method described in paragraph 7.77 because, for a multi-national group comprising operations with a number of functional currencies, it means that the operations can be translated into the presentation currency directly without having to determine a 'functional currency' for the group first. The method also results in the same amounts in the presentation currency regardless of whether the financial statements of a foreign operation are first translated into the functional currency of the parent and then into the presentation currency or translated directly into the presentation currency. [IAS 21 para BC18].

Determining the average rate for translating the income statement

7.81 The standard permits a foreign operation's income statement to be translated at an average rate for the period. IAS 21 does not prescribe any definitive method of calculating the average rate, probably because the appropriate method may justifiably vary between individual entities. For further information refer to paragraphs 7.52 and 7.53 above.

Change in presentation currency

7.82 IAS 21 allows entities a free choice of the currency in which they present their financial statements. [IAS 21 para 38]. The question, therefore, arises how a change in presentation currency should be treated. An entity may choose to change its presentation currency when there is a change in its functional currency, although this is not required (see para 7.46.1). The choice of presentation currency represents an accounting policy and any change should be applied fully

© 2013 PricewaterhouseCoopers LLP. All rights reserved.

的改变。这些汇兑差额确实对可能通过出售或清算实现的净投资有影响，但该影响只与净投资有关而与被投资方的经营无关。因此，将其视作损益是不适当的；从而，其应确认为其他综合收益的一个单独组成部分。

7.80 IASB 选用第 7.77 段中所述的折算方法是因为，对于一个由使用多种功能货币的多个经营构成的跨国集团来说，这意味着各经营可以直接折算为列报货币，而无须先确定集团的“功能货币”。不管境外经营的财务报表是先折算为母公司的功能货币然后再折算为列报货币，还是直接折算为列报货币，该方法也使得按列报货币表示的金额是一致的。[IAS 21 BC 第 18 段]。

确定折算利润表采用的平均汇率

7.81 准则允许以当期平均汇率折算境外经营的利润表。IAS 21 并未规定任何计算平均汇率的确切方法，这很可能是因为个别主体所适用的方法可能因具体情况而不同。参见上文第 7.52 段和第 7.53 段的进一步讨论。

列报货币的变更

7.82 IAS 21 允许主体自由选择列报其财务报表的货币。[IAS 21 第 38 段]。因此，产生了如何处理列报货币变更的问题。当功能货币变更时主体可能选择变更其列报货币，尽管准则没有要求这么做（参见第 7.46.1 段）。列报货币的选择属于一项会计政策，其任何变更均应当遵循 IAS 8 适用完全追溯调整法，除非该方法不切实可行。这意味着变更应当视同于新的列报货币为该主体一直使用的列报货币，且比较数据应以新的列报货币进行重述。由于使用

ⓒ 2013 普华永道（PricewaterhouseCoopers）版权所有。

retrospectively in accordance with IAS 8, unless impracticable. This means that the change should be treated as if the new presentation currency had always been the entity's presentation currency, with comparative amounts being restated into the new presentation currency. Since using a presentation currency is purely applying a translation method, and does not affect the underlying functional currency of the entity or any entities within a group, it is straightforward to apply a change in presentation currency to assets, liabilities and income statement items. All assets and liabilities are translated from their functional currency into the new presentation currency at the beginning of the comparative period using the opening exchange rate and retranslated at the closing rate. Income statement items are translated at an actual rate or at an average rate approximating the actual rate.

7.82.1 However, for the individual items within equity, the process can be more complex. Management has a choice of translating these equity items from an entity's functional currency into its presentation currency at either the closing rate or at the historical rate, with the balancing amount being reported in CTA (see para 7.77.1). Retained earnings, CTA and similar reserves should be expressed in the new presentation currency as if it had always been the presentation currency, unless it is impracticable to do so (see further para 7.82.4).

7.82.2 A change in presentation currency is less problematic where a stand-alone entity (or a group with no foreign operations) reports equity at the closing rate, as it means that some of the CTA that would have arisen on retranslation of net assets will be offset by CTA on retranslation of equity items. CTA will, however, arise as a result of differences between the historical average and closing exchange rates when applied to profit or loss and other performance statement items.

7.82.3 Where equity items are translated at the historical rate and/or where a group has foreign operations, the individual equity items should also be re-expressed in the new presentation currency on a change of presentation currency as if it had always been the presentation currency. [IAS 8 para 19]. This requires determining the amount of each individual equity balance on each earlier reporting date. For unvarying items of equity such as share capital and premium, this may not be too difficult, although even this may be complicated by share issues and buy-backs in different reporting periods.

© 2013 PricewaterhouseCoopers LLP. All rights reserved.

列报货币仅仅是应用一种折算方法，并且不影响主体或集团内任何主体相关的功能货币，所以将列报货币的变更应用于各项资产、负债和利润表项目是直接明确的。所有的资产和负债应于比较期间的期初以期初汇率从功能货币折算为新的列报货币，再以期末汇率进行重新折算。利润表项目以实际汇率或近似于实际汇率的平均汇率进行折算。

7.82.1 然而，对于权益内部的个别项目而言，该过程可能会更加复杂。管理层可以选择以期末汇率或历史汇率将这些权益项目从主体的功能货币折算为其列报货币，并将余额计入 CTA（参见第 7.77.1 段）。留存收益、CTA 和类似的准备金应当以新的列报货币列报，如同该货币一直是列报货币，除非不切实可行（参见下文第 7.82.4 段）。

7.82.2 在某一独立主体（或没有境外经营的集团）以期末汇率列报其权益项目的情况下，变更列报货币带来的问题较少，因为这意味着因净资产折算而产生的部分 CTA 与因权益项目折算而产生的 CTA 相互抵销。然而，因历史平均汇率与期末汇率的不同，损益项目及其他业绩报表项目的折算将产生 CTA。

7.82.3 在权益项目以历史汇率折算及/或某一集团拥有境外经营的情况下，列报货币变更时，每一个别权益项目也应当以新的列报货币重述，如同该货币一直是列报货币。[IAS 8 第 19 段]。这就要求确定每一个别权益项目在其每一较早报告日的金额。对于未发生变动的权益项目诸如股本和股本溢价，这可能并不十分困难，尽管在不同的报告期间发行和回购股份可能使问题复杂化。

© 2013 普华永道（PricewaterhouseCoopers）版权所有。

7.82.4 However, for retained earnings and other similar reserves, the amounts in functional currencies must be translated at the transaction dates with a resulting impact on the amount recognised in CTA. Calculating the split between retained earnings and CTA may be onerous in practice. How difficult will be influenced by whether average rates can be used as an approximation for actual rates, the period over which these changes are to be calculated as well as the number of transactions. It will usually be relatively straightforward to go back as far as the opening balance sheet of the first period presented. The effect of going back further (which will affect only the relative amounts reported in CTA and retained earnings), may not be material, although this will depend on factors such as:

- The size of assets and liabilities.
- The stability of the relevant exchange rates.
- Legal requirements around distributability of profits.
- The reclassification of the deferred foreign exchange gains and losses on the ultimate disposal of a foreign operation.

7.82.5 Where an entity, on adopting IFRS, took the exemption to reset the CTA to zero, we believe that it would not be necessary to restate beyond its transition date (see chapter 2).

7.82.6 In the case where an entity changes its presentation currency, it should present an additional balance sheet in accordance with paragraph 10(f) of IAS 1. See further chapter 4.

Consolidated financial statements

Translation of a foreign operation

7.83 Translating foreign currency financial statements into the presentation currency is necessary so that the foreign operation's financial statements may be included in the reporting entity's financial statements by consolidation, proportional consolidation or the equity method. The method of translation in consolidated financial statements reflects the financial and other operational relationships that

© 2013 PricewaterhouseCoopers LLP. All rights reserved.

7.82.4　然而，对于留存收益及其他类似准备金，功能货币的金额必须于交易日进行折算，并影响确认于 CTA 的金额。实务中分别计算留存收益与 CTA 可能是繁琐的，该难度受平均汇率是否可作为实际汇率的近似汇率使用、计算这些变更的期间以及交易量的影响。追溯到列报的首个期间的期初资产负债表通常相对直接，进一步追溯的影响（仅影响在 CTA 和留存收益中列报的相对金额）可能是不重要的，尽管这将取决于如下因素：

- 资产和负债的规模。
- 相关汇率的稳定性。
- 利润分配能力相关的法律要求。
- 最终处置境外经营时产生的递延汇兑损益的重分类。

7.82.5　在主体采用 IFRS 时使用了将 CTA 重置为零的豁免的情况下，我们认为应该是不需要对转换日之前的金额进行重述（参见第二章）。

7.82.6　在主体变更其列报货币的情形下，应当按照 IAS 1 第 10（f）段列报一份额外的资产负债表。参见第四章的进一步讨论。

合并财务报表

境外经营的折算

7.83　将外币财务报表折算为列报货币是必须的，以便可能可以通过合并、比例合并或权益法将该境外经营的财务报表包括在报告主体的财务报表中。合并财务报表中的折算方法要反映了存在于报告主体与其境外企业之间的财务和其他经营关系。遵循第 7.77 段所述的期末汇率/净投资法可达到该目标。这一折算方法通过下面的示例予以说明。一旦境外经营的财务报表被折算为

ⓒ 2013 普华永道（PricewaterhouseCoopers）版权所有。

exist between the reporting entity and its foreign enterprises. This objective is achieved by following the closing rate/net investment method described in paragraph 7. 77. This translation method is illustrated by the example below. Once the foreign operation's financial statements have been translated into the reporting entity's presentation currency, its incorporation into the reporting entity's consolidated financial statement follows normal consolidation procedures.

Example 1 – Translation of a foreign subsidiary

Entity A, a UK entity, whose accounting period ended on 30 September 20X5, has a wholly-owned US subsidiary, S corporation, which was acquired for US $ 500, 000 on 30 September 20X4. The fair value of the net assets at the date of acquisition was US $ 400, 000 giving rise to goodwill of US $ 100, 000. The exchange rate at 30 September 20X4 and 20X5 was £ 1 = US $ 2. 0 and £ 1 = US $ 1. 5 respectively. The weighted average rate for the year ended 30 September 20X5 was £ 1 = US $ 1. 65. During the year, S corporation paid a dividend of US $ 14, 000 when the rate of exchange was £ 1 = US $ 1. 75.

The foreign currency movements in this example have been exaggerated. In reality, if exchange rates were this volatile, an entity would not be permitted to use average rates for translating the income statement. [IAS 21 para 40].

The summarised income statement of S corporation for the year ended 30 September 20X5, and the summarised balance sheets at 30 September 20X4 and 20X5 in dollars and sterling equivalents, are as follows:

S corporation: Income statement for the year ended 30 September 20X5

	$ '000	**Exchange rate**	**£ '000**
Operating profit	135	1.65	81.8
Interest paid	(15)	1.65	(9.0)
Profit before taxation	120		72.8
Taxation	(30)	1.65	(18.2)
Profit after taxation	90		54.6

© 2013 PricewaterhouseCoopers LLP. All rights reserved.

报告主体的列报货币，其并入报告主体合并财务报表应遵循正常的合并程序。

示例 1——境外子公司的折算

某一英国主体 A，其会计期间为截至 20X5 年 9 月 30 日止年度。其拥有一家美国的全资子公司，S 公司。S 公司是于 20X4 年 9 月 30 日被 A 公司以 500,000 美元收购的。购买日 S 公司净资产的公允价值为 400,000 美元，由此产生 100,000 美元的商誉。20X4 年及 20X5 年 9 月 30 日的汇率分别为 1 英镑 =2.0 美元和 1 英镑 =1.5 美元；截至 20X5 年 9 月 30 日止年度的加权平均汇率为 1 英镑 =1.65 美元。S 公司本年度支付了 14,000 美元的股利，支付当日的汇率为 1 英镑 =1.75 美元。

本例中的外币波动被夸大了。实际上，如果汇率波动如此巨大，主体应该是不被允许使用平均汇率来折算利润表的。[IAS 21 第 40 段]。

S 公司以美元及等价英镑列示的截至 20X4 年 9 月 30 日止年度的汇总利润表及 20X4 年 9 月 30 日、20X5 年 9 月 30 日的汇总资产负债表如下：

S 公司：截至 20X5 年 9 月 30 日止年度利润表

	千美元	汇率	千英镑
营业利润	135	1.65	81.8
利息支出	(15)	1.65	(9.0)
税前利润	120		72.8
所得税	(30)	1.65	(18.2)
税后利润	90		54.6

ⓒ 2013 普华永道（PricewaterhouseCoopers）版权所有。

Balance sheets of S corporation

	20X5	20X4	20X5	20X4
	$ '000	$ '000	£ '000	£ '000
Closing exchange rate £1 =			$1. 50	$2. 00
Property, plant and equipment				
Cost (20X5 additions: $30)	255	225	170. 0	112. 5
Depreciation (20X5 charge: $53)	98	45	65. 3	22. 5
Net book value	157	180	104. 7	90. 0
Current assets:				
Inventories	174	126	116. 0	63. 0
Debtors	210	145	140. 0	72. 5
Cash at bank	240	210	160. 0	105. 0
	624	481	416. 0	240. 5
Current liabilities:				
Trade creditors	125	113	83. 3	57. 5
Taxation	30	18	20. 0	9. 0
	155	131	103. 3	65. 5
Net current assets	469	350	312. 7	175. 0
Loan stock	150	130	100. 0	65. 0
Net assets	476	400	317. 4	200. 0
Share capital	200	200	100. 0	100. 0
Retained profits	276	200	217. 4	100. 0
	476	400	317. 4	200. 0

Analysis of retained profits

	$ '000	£ '000
Pre-acquisition profit brought forward	200	100. 0
Profit for the year	90	54. 6
Dividends paid in the year *	(14)	(8. 0)
Exchange difference	–	70. 8
Retained profits	276	217. 4

* Dividend paid during the year is translated at the actual rate $1 = £ 1. 75

© 2013 PricewaterhouseCoopers LLP. All rights reserved.

S 公司资产负债表

	20X5 年 千美元	20X4 年 千美元	20X5 年 千英镑	20X4 年 千英镑
期末汇率 1 英镑 =			1.50 美元	2.00 美元
不动产、工厂及设备				
成本（20X5 年新增：30 美元）	255	225	170.0	112.5
折旧（20X5 年计提：53 美元）	98	45	65.3	22.5
账面净值	157	180	104.7	90.0
流动资产：				
存货	174	126	116.0	63.0
应收款	210	145	140.0	72.5
银行存款	240	210	160.0	105.0
	624	481	416.0	240.5
流动负债：				
应付账款	125	113	83.3	57.5
税金	30	18	20.0	9.0
	155	131	103.3	65.5
流动资产净额	469	350	312.7	175.0
贷款	150	130	100.0	65.0
净资产	476	400	317.4	200.0
股本	200	200	100.0	100.0
留存收益	276	200	217.4	100.0
	476	400	317.4	200.0

留存收益分析

	千美元	千英镑
购买前结转的利润	200	100.0
本年利润	90	54.6
本年支付的股利*	（14）	（8.0）
汇兑差额	–	70.8
留存收益	276	217.4

* 本年支付的股利以实际汇率 1 美元 = 1.75 英镑折算

ⓒ 2013 普华永道（PricewaterhouseCoopers）版权所有。

Analysis of exchange difference:

Arising on retranslation of opening net assets (excluding goodwill – see below)	
at opening rate – $400,000 @ $2 = £1	200.0
at closing rate – $400,000 @ $1.5 = £1	266.7
Exchange gain on net assets	66.7
Exchange gain arising from translating retained profits from average to closing rate – $90,000 @1.5 – £54,600	5.4
Exchange loss arising from translating dividend from actual to closing rate – $14,000 @1.5 – £8,000	(1.3)
Total exchange difference arising on translation of S corporation	70.8
Exchange difference on goodwill of US $100,000 treated as a currency asset (see para 7.86 below)	
at opening rate – US $100,000 @ $2 = £1	50.0
at closing rate – US $100,000 @ $1.5 = £1	66.7
Exchange gain on goodwill included in consolidation	16.7
Total exchange difference included in consolidated balance sheet as a separate component of equity (see below)	87.5

It is assumed that parent entity A's functional currency is the pound sterling. It has received a dividend from S corporation during the year. The summarised balance sheets of entity A at 30 September 20X4 and 20X5 are as follows:

Entity A – Balance sheets	**20X5**	**20X4**
	£'000	**£'000**
Investments in subsidiary S ($500,000 @ 2.0)	250	250
Cash	208	200
Net assets	458	450
Share capital	450	450
Retained profits (dividend received: $14,000 @ 1.75*)	8	–
	458	450

* actual rate on date dividend received

© 2013 PricewaterhouseCoopers LLP. All rights reserved.

汇兑差额分析：

由期初净资产（不含商誉——参见以下分析）重新折算产生：

以期初汇率折算——400,000 美元以期初汇率 2 折算	200.0
以期末汇率折算——400,000 美元以期末汇率 1.5 折算	266.7
净资产汇兑收益	66.7
以期末汇率折算与以平均汇率折算税后利润而产生的汇兑收益——US90,000/1.5 – £54,600	5.4
以实际汇率折算与以期末汇率折算股利而产生的汇兑损失——US14,000/1.5 – £8,000	(1.3)
因 S 公司折算而产生的汇兑差额合计	70.8
被视为货币资产的 100,000 美元的商誉产生的汇兑差额（参见下文第 7.86 段）	
以期初汇率折算——100,000 美元按期初汇率 2 折算	50.0
以期末汇率折算——100,000 美元按期末汇率 1.5 折算	66.7
合并报表中商誉所产生的汇兑收益	16.7
合并资产负债表中列示为权益的单独项目的汇兑差额总额（参见下表）	87.5

假设母公司 A 的功能货币为英镑，并于本年度收到 S 公司支付的股利。主体 A 于 20X4 年及 20X5 年 9 月 30 日的汇总资产负债表列示如下：

主体 A——资产负债表	**20X5 年**	**20X4 年**
	千英镑	**千英镑**
对子公司 S 的投资（500,000 美元按汇率 2.0 折算）	250	250
现金	208	200
净资产	458	450
股本	450	450
留存收益（收到的股利：14,000 美元按汇率 1.75* 折算）	8	–
	458	450

* 收到股利当日的实际汇率

ⓒ 2013 普华永道（PricewaterhouseCoopers）版权所有。

The summarised consolidated income statement for the year ended 30 September 20X5 and the consolidated balance sheet as at date prepared under the closing rate/net investment method are as follows:

Consolidated income statement for the year ended 30 September 20X5

	£'000
Operating profit of S corporation	81.8
Operating profit of entity A	8.0
	89.8
Elimination of inter-company dividend*	(8.0)
Net operating profit	81.8
Interest paid	(9.0)
Profit before taxation	72.8
Taxation	(18.2)
Retained profit	54.6

Consolidated balance sheet as at 30 September 20X5

	£'000
Goodwill	66.7
Property, plant and equipment	104.7
	171.4
Current assets:	
Inventories	116.0
Debtors	140.0
Cash (S corporation: £160; entity A £208)	368.0
	624.0
Current liabilities:	
Trade creditors	83.3
Taxation	20.0
	103.3
Net current assets	520.7
Loan stock	100.0
Net assets	592.1

© 2013 PricewaterhouseCoopers LLP. All rights reserved.

根据期末汇率/净投资法编制的截至20X5年9月30日止年度汇总合并利润表及该日合并资产负债表列示如下：

截至20X5年9月30日止年度合并利润表

	千英镑
S公司的营业利润	81.8
主体A的营业利润	8.0
	89.8
集团内股利的抵销*	(8.0)
营业利润净额	81.8
已付利息	(9.0)
税前利润	72.8
所得税	(18.2)
留存收益	54.6

截至20X5年9月30日合并资产负债表

	千英镑
商誉	66.7
不动产、工厂及设备	104.7
	171.4
流动资产：	
存货	116.0
应收款项	140.0
现金（S公司：160英镑；主体A：208英镑）	368.0
	624.0
流动负债：	
应付账款	83.3
税金	20.0
	103.3
流动资产净额	520.7
贷款	100.0
净资产	592.1

ⓒ 2013 普华永道（PricewaterhouseCoopers）版权所有。

Capital and reserves	
Share capital	450. 0
Retained profit	54. 6
Cumulative translation adjustment	87. 5
	592. 1

Different reporting dates

7. 84 Where a foreign subsidiary's financial statements are drawn up to a date that is different from that of the parent, the foreign subsidiary often prepares additional financial statements as of the same date as the parent for inclusion in the parent's financial statements. Therefore, the foreign subsidiary's financial statements are translated at the exchange rate at the parent's balance sheet date. Where additional financial statements are not prepared, IAS 27 allows the use of a different reporting date that is not more than three months before or three months after the reporting entity's balance sheet date. The foreign subsidiary's financial statements are translated at the exchange rate ruling at the foreign operation's balance sheet date. However, if significant transactions or events occur between the date of the subsidiary's financial statements and the date of the parent's financial statements, adjustments are made. [IAS 27 para 23]. This may include changes to the exchange rate, as shown in the example below.

Example – Translation of a foreign subsidiary with a different reporting date to that of the parent

Entity A prepares its annual financial statements at 31 January. However, local regulations require one of its subsidiaries, entity B, to prepare its financial statements at 31 December. Entity A uses entity B's results for the 12 months to 31 December for consolidation purposes, rather than have a second set of results audited to 31 January.

The exchange rate between the US dollar (used for group reporting) and entity B's local currency was US $ 1: LC15, 000 at 31 December 20X2 and US $ 1: LC18, 000 at 31 January 20X3. There were no significant transactions or other events at entity B during January 20X3. Entity B's net assets at 31

© 2013 PricewaterhouseCoopers LLP. All rights reserved.

资本及准备	
股本	450.0
留存收益	54.6
累计折算调整	87.5
	592.1

不同的报告日

7.84 在境外子公司财务报表的截止日与母公司不同的情况下，境外子公司经常编制一份额外的、与母公司报表日相同的财务报表，以便并入母公司的财务报表。因此，境外子公司的财务报表以母公司资产负债表日的汇率进行折算。在子公司没有编制额外财务报表的情况下，IAS 27 允许使用不同的报告日（与报告主体的资产负债表日前后相差不超过三个月）。此时，境外子公司的财务报表以该境外经营资产负债表日的汇率进行折算。然而，如果在子公司的报告日与母公司的报告日之间发生了重大交易或事项，应进行调整。[IAS 27 第 27 段]。这可能包括如以下示例所述的汇率变动。

示例——与母公司报告日不同的境外子公司的折算

主体于 1 月 31 日编制其年度财务报表。然而子公司之一主体 B 的当地法规要求其于 12 月 31 日编制其年度财务报表。合并时，主体 A 使用主体 B 截至 12 月 31 日的 12 个月的经营成果，而非另一套截至 1 月 31 日的经审计的经营成果。

美元（用于集团报告）与主体 B 的当地货币之间的汇率为：于 20X2 年 12 月 31 日为 1 美元 = 15,000LC；于 20X3 年 1 月 31 日为 1 美元 = 18,000LC。20X3 年 1 月间主体 B 没有发生重大交易或其他事项。主体 B 于 20X2 年 12 月 31 日的净资产为 234,000,000LC。

ⓒ 2013 普华永道（PricewaterhouseCoopers）版权所有。

December 20X2 were LC234 million.

The net assets of entity B at 31 December 20X2 using the exchange rate of 31 December 20X2 are US $ 15,600.

The change in exchange rates between 31 December 20X2 and 31 January 20X3 is significant. Therefore, entity A uses the exchange rate of 31 January 20X3 for consolidation purposes.

Accordingly, management should translate entity B's balance sheet as at 31 December 20X2 using the 31 January 20X3 exchange rate. This results in the consolidation of a balance sheet with net assets of US $ 13, 000.

The same approach is used for foreign associates and joint ventures. [IAS 21 para 46].

Equity Items

7. 84. 1 The standard is silent on how to translate equity items. Management, therefore, has a choice of using either the historical rate or the closing rate. The chosen policy should be applied consistently. If the closing rate is used, the resulting exchange differences are recognised in equity; the policy choice, therefore, has no impact on the amount of total equity. The regulatory framework in some jurisdictions may mandate one treatment. In this case, the policy choice does not apply.

Non-controlling interest

7. 85 Exchange differences arising on the retranslation of a foreign subsidiary's financial statements are recognised in other comprehensive income and accumulated as a separate component of equity. Where the foreign subsidiary is not wholly-owned, the exchange differences that are attributable to the non-controlling interest are allocated to, and reported as part of, the non-controlling interest in the consolidated balance sheet. [IAS 21 para 41].

© 2013 PricewaterhouseCoopers LLP. All rights reserved.

主体 B 于 20X2 年 12 月 31 日的净资产以当日汇率折算为 15,600 美元。

20X2 年 12 月 31 日与 20X3 年 1 月 31 日之间的汇率变动时重大的。因此，为了合并主体 A 使用 20X3 年 1 月 31 日的汇率。

相应地，管理层应当使用 20X3 年 1 月 31 日的汇率折算主体 B 截至 20X2 年 12 月 31 日的资产负债表。这使得合并净资产为 13,000 美元的资产负债表。

同样的方法适用于折算境外联营和合营。[IAS 21 第 46 段]。

权益项目

7.84.1 准则未提及如何折算权益项目。因此，管理层可以选择使用历史汇率或期末汇率。所选择的政策应当一致地应用。如果使用期末汇率，产生的汇兑差额确认于权益；因此，会计政策选择对于权益总额没有影响。在某些管辖区内的法规框架可能强制要求一种处理方式。在这种情形下，会计政策选择不适用。

非控制性权益

7.85 境外子公司财务报表重新折算所产生的汇兑差额应确认于其他综合收益，并作为权益中的一个单独组成部分予以累计。在境外子公司并非全资拥有的情况下，归属于非控制性权益的汇兑差额将在合并资产负债表中分配至非控制性权益，并作为其组成部分进行报告。[IAS 21 第 41 段]。

© 2013 普华永道（PricewaterhouseCoopers）版权所有。

Goodwill and fair value adjustments arising on an acquisition

7. 86 Goodwill arising in a business combination is measured as the excess of the consideration transferred for the combination over the acquirer's interest in the net fair value of the acquiree's identifiable assets and liabilities and any non-controlling interest.

7. 87 Goodwill and fair value adjustments form part of the acquired entity's assets and liabilities.

- Any goodwill arising on the acquisition of a foreign operation and any fair value adjustments to the carrying amounts of assets and liabilities arising on a foreign operation's acquisition are treated as the foreign operation's assets and liabilities.

- They are expressed in the foreign operation's functional currency and are translated at the closing rate in accordance with paragraphs 7. 77 above, where the functional currency is not the currency of a hyper-inflationary economy, and in accordance with paragraph 7. 109 below, where the functional currency is the currency of a hyper-inflationary economy.

[IAS 21 para 47].

7. 88 Therefore, where a parent entity acquires a multinational operation comprising businesses with many different functional currencies, the goodwill arising on acquisition is allocated to the level of each functional currency of the acquired foreign operation. This means that the level at which goodwill is allocated for foreign currency translation purposes may be different from the level at which goodwill is tested for impairment in accordance with IAS 36. [IAS 36 para 83].

Example – Translation of goodwill and fair value adjustments

On 30 June 20X5, a UK parent entity with sterling as the functional currency acquired a multinational group with operations in Canada, the US and Europe. All foreign operations are highly profitable. The functional currencies of the foreign operations are their respective local currencies. The total purchase consideration amounted to £3, 000 million. The UK parent financial year ends on 31 December 20X5.

© 2013 PricewaterhouseCoopers LLP. All rights reserved.

购买产生的商誉和公允价值调整

7.86　业务合并产生的商誉是以合并所转移的对价高于购买方所享有的被购买方可辨认资产和负债以及任何非控制性权益的净公允价值部分进行计量的。

7.87　商誉和公允价值调整构成被购买主体资产及负债的一部分。

- 购买境外经营产生的商誉以及由于购买该境外经营产生的对资产和负债的账面价值所进行的公允价值调整，视作该境外经营的资产与负债。

- 其以境外经营的功能货币表示，在境外经营的功能货币为非恶性通货膨胀经济中的货币的情况下，根据上文第 7.77 段以期末汇率进行折算；在该功能货币为恶性通货膨胀经济中的货币的情况下，则按照下文第 7.109 段以期末汇率进行折算。

[IAS 21 第 47 段]。

7.88　因此，在母公司购买一个跨国经营且该跨国经营包括多个不同功能货币的业务的情况下，因购买而产生的商誉应分配至被收购境外经营的每一功能货币水平。这意味着，为外币折算目的进行商誉分摊的水平可能与按照 IAS 36 对商誉进行减值测试的水平不同。[IAS 36 第 83 段]。

示例——商誉和公允价值调整的折算

某一以英镑为功能货币的英国母公司于 20X5 年 6 月 30 日购买了一个在加拿大、美国和欧洲拥有经营的跨国集团。所有的境外经营均有高盈利，其功能货币分别为各自的当地货币。购买对价总额为 3,000,000 英镑。该英国母公司的会计年度结束于 20X5 年 12 月 31 日。

ⓒ 2013 普华永道（PricewaterhouseCoopers）版权所有。

The fair values of the net assets of the acquired businesses, including fair value adjustments and the relevant exchange rates at the date of acquisition and at the balance sheet date, are given below. The UK parent allocates the purchased goodwill to the acquired businesses on the basis of their relative adjusted fair values of the net assets acquired.

Business acquired	**Canada**	**US**	**Europe**	**Total**
Exchange rate at acquisition £1 =	2.19	1.66	1.42	
Exchange rate at balance sheet date £1 =	2.29	1.80	1.45	
	C $ '000	**$ '000**	**€ '000**	**£ '000**
Net assets – book value	1,200	1,500	2,000	
Fair value adjustments	150	50	(100)	
Adjusted fair values	1,350	1,550	1,900	
Allocation of goodwill				
Translated at exchange rate at date of acquisition	£616	£934	£1,338	2,888
Purchase consideration				3,000
Goodwill allocated on the basis of adjusted fair values	£24	£36	£52	112
	C $ '000	**$ '000**	**€ '000**	
Adjusted net assets as above	1,350	1,550	1,900	
Goodwill treated as currency asset	53	60	74	
Adjusted fair value + goodwill	1,403	1,610	1,974	
Translation adjustment on opening net assets	**£ '000**	**£ '000**	**£ '000**	**£ '000**
Adjusted net assets + goodwill @ closing rate	613	894	1,361	2,868
Adjusted net assets + goodwill @ opening rate	640	970	1,390	3,000
Exchange loss taken to other comprehensive income on consolidation	(27)	(76)	(29)	(132)

© 2013 PricewaterhouseCoopers LLP. All rights reserved.

购买的业务的净资产的公允价值（包括公允价值调整）和合并日及资产负债表日的相关汇率列示如下。英国母公司以购买的净资产经过相关调整后的公允价值为基础将购买的商誉分摊至购买的各个业务。

购买的业务	**加拿大**	**美国**	**欧洲**	**合计**
购买日的汇率 1 英镑 =	2.19	1.66	1.42	
资产负债表日的汇率 1 英镑 =	2.29	1.80	1.45	
	千加元	**千美元**	**千欧元**	**千英镑**
净资产——账面价值	1,200	1,500	2,000	
公允价值调整	150	50	（100）	
调整后的公允价值	1,350	1,550	1,900	
商誉的分摊				
以购买日的汇率折算	616 英镑	934 英镑	1,338 英镑	2,888
购买对价				3,000
以调整后的公允价值为基础分摊的商誉	24 英镑	36 英镑	52 英镑	112
	千加元	**千美元**	**千欧元**	
如上调整后的净资产	1,350	1,550	1,900	
视为货币资产的商誉	53	60	74	
调整后的公允价值 + 商誉	1,403	1,610	1,974	
	千英镑	**千英镑**	**千英镑**	**千英镑**
对期初净资产的折算调整				
调整后的净资产 + 商誉按期末汇率折算	613	894	1,361	2,868
调整后的净资产 + 商誉按期初汇率折算	640	970	1,390	3,000
合并报表时计入其他综合收益的汇兑损失	（27）	（76）	（29）	（132）

ⓒ 2013 普华永道（PricewaterhouseCoopers）版权所有。

Consolidated balance sheet at 31 December 20X5

Goodwill at closing rate	23	33	51	107
Net assets at closing rate	590	861	1,310	2,761
Cash outlay				(3,000)
Consolidated net assets				(132)
Translation adjustments in equity	(27)	(76)	(29)	(132)

Intra-group trading transactions

7.89 Where normal trading transactions take place between group companies located in different countries, the transactions give rise to monetary assets (liabilities) that may either have been settled during the year or remain unsettled at the balance sheet date. As the transactions will be recorded in the functional currency of one of the companies in question, exchange differences will arise. These are reported in the entity's income statement in the same way as gains or losses on transactions arising with third parties, as explained from paragraph 7.67 above. Where the monetary asset or liability is settled during the year, the exchange gain or loss will have affected group cash flows. It is, therefore, included in consolidated results for the year. The exchange difference arising simply reflects the risk of doing business with a foreign party, even though that party happens to be a group member. Even where the transaction remains unsettled at the balance sheet date and the monetary asset (liability) in one group entity is eliminated against the corresponding liability (asset) in another group entity, the exchange difference reported in the group entity's own income statement continues to be recognised in consolidated profit or loss. This is because the monetary item represents a commitment to convert one currency into another and exposes the reporting entity to gain or loss through currency fluctuations. [IAS 21 para 45].

Example – Elimination of intra-group trading transactions where the inventory is still owned by the group

A UK parent entity has a wholly-owned subsidiary in the US. During the year ended 31 December 20X5, the US entity purchased plant and raw materials to

© 2013 PricewaterhouseCoopers LLP. All rights reserved.

20X5 年 12 月 31 日合并资产负债表

以期末汇率折算的商誉	23	33	51	107
以期末汇率折算的净资产	590	861	1,310	2,761
现金支出				(3,000)
合并净资产				(132)
计入权益的折算调整	(27)	(76)	(29)	(132)

集团内的供销交易

7.89 在位于不同国家的集团公司间发生正常供销交易的情况下，该交易产生的货币性资产（负债）可能已于当年结算，也可能在资产负债表日仍未结算。由于该交易将以所讨论的公司之一的功能货币记录，因此将产生汇兑差额。该汇兑差额与同第三方交易产生的利得或损失一样报告于主体的利润表（如上文第 7.67 段所述）。在该货币性资产或负债于当年结算的情况下，汇兑损益将已影响集团的现金流；因此包含在当年的合并经营成果中。产生的汇兑差额仅反映了与境外公司做交易的风险，即使对方恰巧是集团成员。即使在资产负债表日该交易仍未结算，且一个集团主体内的货币性资产（负债）与另一集团主体内相应的负债（资产）相互抵销的情况下，报告于该集团主体自身利润表的汇兑差额将继续确认于合并损益中。这是因为货币性项目代表着将一种货币转换成另一种货币的承诺，并使报告主体面临因汇率波动而产生利得或损失的风险。[IAS 21 第 45 段]。

示例——在集团仍持有存货的情况下，集团内供销交易的抵销

某一英国母公司拥有一家位于美国的全资子公司。在截至 20X5 年 12 月 31 日止的年度内，该美国主体从英国母公司处购买了工厂和原材料用于

© 2013 普华永道（PricewaterhouseCoopers）版权所有。

be used in its manufacturing process from the UK parent. Details of the transactions are as follows:

	Exchange rate
Purchased plant costing £500, 000 on 30 April 20X5	£1 = US $ 1. 48
Paid for plant on 30 September 20X5	£1 = US $ 1. 54
Purchased raw materials costing £300, 000 on 31 October 20X5	£1 = US $ 1. 56
Balance of £300, 000 outstanding at 31 December 20X5	£1 = US $ 1. 52
Average rate for the year	£1 = US $ 1. 55

The following exchange gains/losses will be recorded in the US subsidiary's income statement for the year ended 31 December 20X5.

	US $	**US $**
Plant costing £500,000 @ 1.48	740,000	
Paid £500,000 @ 1.54	770,000	
Exchange loss – settled transaction		(30,000)
Raw materials costing £300,000 @ 1.56	468,000	
Outstanding £300,000 @ 1.52	456,000	
Exchange gain – unsettled transaction		12,000
Net exchange loss recorded in income statement		(18,000)

The exchange loss of US $ 30, 000 that arises as the inter-company payable for plant purchase is settled during the year will flow through on consolidation when the US subsidiary's results are incorporated in the consolidated financial statements. The inter-company payable of US $ 456, 000 in the US subsidiary's balance sheet that remains outstanding will be translated into sterling at the closing rate to £300, 000 and will be eliminated against the receivable recorded in the UK parent's inter-company account.

© 2013 PricewaterhouseCoopers LLP. All rights reserved.

其生产过程。交易明细如下：

	汇率
于 20X5 年 4 月 30 日购买的工厂成本为 500,000 英镑	1 英镑 = 1.48 美元
于 20X5 年 9 月 30 日支付的工厂款项	1 英镑 = 1.54 美元
于 20X5 年 10 月 31 日购买的原材料成本为 300,000 英镑	1 英镑 = 1.56 美元
于 20X5 年 12 月 31 日仍未结算的款项余额为 300,000 英镑	1 英镑 = 1.52 美元
当年平均汇率	1 英镑 = 1.55 美元

下列汇兑收益/损失将计入美国子公司截至 20X5 年 12 月 31 日止年度的利润表内。

	美元	美元
工厂成本：500,000 英镑按汇率 1.48 折算	740,000	
已支付：500,000 英镑按汇率 1.54 折算	770,000	
汇兑损失—已结算的交易		(30,000)
原材料成本：300,000 英镑按汇率 1.56 折算	468,000	
未结算的款项：300,000 英镑按汇率 1.52 折算	456,000	
汇兑收益—未结算的交易		12,000
计入利润表的汇兑净损失		(18,000)

由于公司之间购买工厂的应付款项于当年结算而产生的汇兑损失 30,000 美元，将在该美国子公司的经营成果纳入合并报表时流向合并报表。该美国子公司的资产负债表中尚未结算的公司之间应付款项 456,000 美元将以期末汇率折算为 300,000 英镑，并将与英国母公司的公司之间账户内记录的应收款项相抵销。

ⓒ 2013 普华永道（PricewaterhouseCoopers）版权所有。

However, the exchange gain of US $12,000 will not be eliminated on consolidation and will be reported as part of the consolidated results of the group. The rationale of keeping this gain in the group's result is that to repay the payable balance, the US subsidiary will some day have to expend the amount of its local currency necessary to acquire the required amount of the reporting currency. This exposes the group to a gain or loss on reconversion.

7.90 The same treatment that applies to an unsettled inter-company monetary item arising from trading transactions also applies to intra-group loans made by one group member to another in a currency that is different from the borrower's functional currency. That is, the borrower will initially record the foreign currency loan at the rate of exchange ruling at the date the loan is made. At each balance sheet date thereafter, until it is repaid, the loan will be translated at the closing rate and any exchange difference will be reported in the borrower's income statement. On consolidation, the intra-group loan account will cancel out, but the exchange difference reported in the borrower's income statement continues to be recognised in profit or loss.

Unrealised profit on inventories

7.91 IAS 27requires intra-group profit arising from the transfer of assets between entities in the group to be eliminated in full in the group accounts where such assets are still held in the undertakings included in the consolidation at the balance sheet date. This is because it does not represent profit to the group (see further chapter 24). No specific guidance is given in IAS 21 as to the exchange rate at which the profit should be eliminated. However, US GAAP requires elimination at the actual rate ruling at the transaction date or at a weighted average rate (Codification para 830-30-45-10).

Example – Elimination of intra-group trading transactions where the inventory had been sold outside the group

The facts are the same as in the example in paragraph 7.89 except that the raw materials purchased for £300,000 by the US subsidiary are still in inventory at 31 December 20X5. These goods cost the UK parent £270,000.

© 2013 PricewaterhouseCoopers LLP. All rights reserved.

然而，在合并报表时，汇兑收益 12,000 美元将不会被抵销，并作为集团合并经营成果的一部分进行列报。将该收益保留在集团经营成果中的理由是因为美国子公司为了偿还该应付款项，未来某日将必须支付购买所要求金额的报告货币所必需的当地货币金额。这使得集团面临因货币再转换产生的利得或损失的风险。

7.90 适用于供销交易产生的公司之间尚未结算的货币性项目的会计处理，也同样适用于由集团内某一成员向另一成员提供的、以不同于借款方功能货币的货币计价的集团内贷款。即，该借款方将以贷款发放当日的汇率初始记录该外币贷款。在此后的每一个资产负债表日，该贷款将以期末汇率进行折算，任何汇兑差额将报告于借款方的利润表，直至贷款偿还。合并报表时，该集团内贷款账户将抵销，但报告于借款方利润表中的汇兑差额仍继续确认于损益。

存货中的未实现利润

7.91 IAS 27 要求集团内各个主体之间转移资产所产生的集团内利润，在资产负债表日该资产仍然由合并范围内的企业所持有的情况下，应在集团报表中全额抵销。这是因为其并不代表集团的利润（参见第二十四章的进一步讨论）。IAS 21 没有提供该利润应当以何种利率予以抵销的明确指引。然而，US GAAP 要求以交易当日的实际汇率或加权平均汇率进行抵销（汇编第 830-30-45-10）。

示例——在存货尚未销往集团外部的情况下集团内供销交易的抵销

事实情况与第 7.89 段的例子相同，但美国子公司以 300,000 英镑购买的原材料在 20X5 年 12 月 31 日仍为存货。这些商品在英国母公司的成本为 270,000 英镑。

© 2013 普华永道（PricewaterhouseCoopers）版权所有。

Unrealised profit of £30, 000 (£300, 000 – £270, 000) that the parent entity made on the inter-company sale would, therefore, need to be eliminated on consolidation. However, elimination of this unrealised profit of £30, 000 will not necessarily result in the inventories being included in the consolidated balance sheet at cost to the group where the closing rate method is used, as illustrated below.

The amount for raw materials included in inventory in the US entity's balance sheet at the transaction date is US $468, 000. Under the closing rate method, the inventory would be retranslated at the year end rate of 1. 52 to £307, 895. Therefore, the inventory will be recorded in the consolidated balance sheet as follows:

	£
Cost of inventory US $468, 000 @ 1. 52	307,895
Unrealised profit	(30, 000)
Inventory carried in consolidated balance sheet	277,895

The difference of £7,895 represents the exchange difference arising on the retranslation of the inventory in the subsidiary's financial statements to the year end rate under the closing rate/net investment method – that is, £307, 895 less the cost to the subsidiary of £300, 000.

If the parent has purchased the raw materials from the US subsidiary for US 468, 000 at 31 October 20X5, which cost the US subsidiary US $421,200, and these items were still in the parent's inventory at the year end, a problem arises as to what rate the unrealised profit of US $46,800 is eliminated.

As stated above, if the guidance in US GAAP is followed, the profit will be eliminated at the actual rate ruling at the transaction date. The inventory will be recorded in the consolidated balance sheet as follows:

	£
Cost of inventory US $468, 000 @1. 56	300, 000
Unrealised profit US $46,800 @1. 56	(30, 000)
Inventory carried in consolidated balance sheet	270, 000

The amount of inventory recorded in the balance sheet represents the original cost

© 2013 PricewaterhouseCoopers LLP. All rights reserved.

因此，母公司就公司之间的销售取得的未实现利润 30,000 英镑（300,000 英镑 – 270,000 英镑）应该是需要在合并报表时予以抵销的。然而，在采用期末汇率法的情况下，抵销未实现利润 30,000 英镑并不一定会使得存货在合并资产负债表中以集团的成本列示，说明如下。

于交易当日，美国主体的资产负债表中包含于存货中的原材料金额为 468,000 美元。根据期末汇率法，该存货应该会以年末汇率 1.52 重新折算为 307,895 英镑。因此，该存货将在合并资产负债表中列示如下：

	英镑
存货成本 468,000 美元按汇率 1.52 折算	307,895
未实现利润	(30,000)
列示于合并资产负债表中的存货	277,895

7,895 英镑的差额代表子公司资产负债表中的存货根据期末汇率/净投资法以期末汇率重新折算产生的汇兑差额，即 307,895 英镑减去子公司的购买成本 300,000 英镑。

如果母公司于 20X5 年 10 月 31 日以 468,000 美元的价格从美国子公司购买成本为 421,200 美元的原材料，并且这些货物于年底仍在母公司的存货中，这将产生一个未实现利润 46,800 美元以何种汇率予以抵销的问题。

如上所述，若遵循 US GAAP 的规定，该利润将以交易日的实际汇率进行抵销。该存货将在合并资产负债表中进行如下记录：

	英镑
存货成本 468,000 美元按汇率 1.56 折算	300,000
未实现利润 46,800 美元按汇率 1.56 折算	(30,000)
列示于合并资产负债表中的存货	270,000

在资产负债表中记录的存货金额代表集团的初始成本 421,200 美元以集

ⓒ 2013 普华永道（PricewaterhouseCoopers）版权所有。

to the group of US $421,200 translated at the rate ruling at the date of the intra-group transaction – that is, US $421,200 @ 1.56 = £270,000. This is the method required by US GAAP, which can be applied under IAS 21.

In practice, it is likely that the UK parent will use an average rate for translating the results of foreign operations. The amount of profit to be eliminated is calculated using that average rate. Use of an average rate is permissible where it approximates the exchange rate at the date of the transaction.

	£
Cost of inventory US $468,000 @ 1.56	300,000
Unrealised profit US $46,800 @ 1.55	(30,194)
	269,806

The amount of inventory recorded in the consolidated balance sheet under the closing rate/net investment method will not be the same as the actual cost to the group.

7.92 Even if intra-group transactions do not give rise to intra-group profit, there could still be an effect on asset values, as the following example illustrates.

Example – Intra-group trading transaction at cost

A UK parent has a wholly-owned subsidiary in Pololand. The currency is Pol. The net assets of the group at 31 March 20X5 are £54,000, consisting of cash £24,000, held in the UK parent and inventory held in the Pololand subsidiary costing Pol 3m. This was included in the consolidated balance sheet at the closing rate of £1 = Pol 100. On 30 September 20X5, the subsidiary transfers the goods to its UK parent at cost price when the rate of exchange is £1 = Pol 125. The transaction is settled in cash, and the goods are included in the parent's inventory at £24,000. At 31 March 20X6, the goods are still in inventory. The Pol has weakened further against sterling and the exchange rate at the balance sheet date is £1 = Pol 150.

No gain or loss is recorded by either entity on the transfer; there are therefore no inter-company profits to be eliminated.

© 2013 PricewaterhouseCoopers LLP. All rights reserved.

团内交易日的汇率折算的金额，即 421,200 美元按汇率 1.56 折算为 270,000 英镑。这是 US GAAP 要求的方法，其在 IAS 21 下可以适用。

在实务中，英国母公司可能会使用平均汇率以折算境外经营的经营成果。予以抵销的利润金额也使用该平均汇率进行计算。在平均汇率近似于交易当日汇率的情况下，允许使用平均汇率。

	英镑
存货成本 468,000 美元按汇率 1.56 折算	300,000
未实现利润 46,800 美元按汇率 1.55 折算	(30,194)
	269,806

根据期末汇率/净投资法，合并资产负债表中记录的存货金额将与集团实际成本不同。

7.92 如下例所示，即使集团内交易未产生集团内利润，仍可能对资产价值产生影响。

示例——以成本进行的集团内供销交易

某英国母公司在 Pololand 有一家全资子公司，货币为 Pol。集团于 20X5 年 3 月 31 日的净资产为 54,000 英镑，其中包括英国母公司持有的现金 24,000 英镑以及 Pololand 子公司持有的成本为 300 万 Pol 的存货。其以期末汇率 1 英镑 = 100Pol 进行折算并包含于合并资产负债表中。于 20X5 年 9 月 30 日，该子公司以成本价将货物转移给英国母公司，转移日汇率为 1 英镑 = 125Pol。该交易以现金结算，且该货物以 24,000 英镑包含于母公司的存货中。于 20X6 年 3 月 31 日，该货物仍在存货中。Pol 相对于英镑进一步贬值，资产负债表日的汇率为 1 英镑 = 150Pol。

两个主体都未因转移而记录损益；因此没有应予抵销的公司之间利润。

ⓒ 2013 普华永道（PricewaterhouseCoopers）版权所有。

		31 March 20X5
		£
Net assets:		
Inventory 3m @ 100 (held by subsidiary)		30,000
Cash (held by parent)		24,000
		54,000

		31 March 20X6
		£
Net assets:		
Inventory (held by parent)		24,000
Cash 3m @ 150 (held by subsidiary)		20,000
		44,000
Exchange difference on retranslation of opening net assets of foreign subsidiary:		
3m @ 100 =	30,000	
3m @ 150 =	20,000	10,000
		54,000

No exchange difference is included in the consolidated income statement, as there is no trading gain or loss. However the effect of switching inventory around the group affects the asset's carrying value. If the inventory had not been transferred, the net assets would still have decreased by £10,000, but the reduction would have been entirely in the inventory value with the cash balance unchanged. However, the result of moving the inventory and cash around the group is that there is a decrease of £6,000 in the inventory value and a decrease of £4,000 in the group's cash position. This reflects the fact that the group's foreign currency exposure is centred on different assets.

Monetary items forming part of net investment in a foreign operation

7.93 The net investment that a reporting entity has in a foreign operation is its interest in the net assets of that operation. [IAS 21 para 8]. In circumstances described in paragraph 7.95 below, a monetary item that is receivable from or

© 2013 PricewaterhouseCoopers LLP. All rights reserved.

		20X5 年 3 月 31 日 英镑
净资产：		
存货 300 万 以汇率 100 折算（由子公司持有）		30, 000
现金（由母公司持有）		24, 000
		54, 000

		20X6 年 3 月 31 日 英镑
净资产：		
存货（由母公司持有）		24, 000
现金 300 万以汇率 150 折算（由子公司持有）		20, 000
		44, 000
重新折算境外子公司期初净资产所产生的汇兑差额：		
300 万以汇率 100 折算 =	30, 000	
300 万以汇率 150 折算 =	20, 000	10, 000
		54, 000

由于没有交易损益，因此合并利润表中没有汇兑差额。然而，集团内交换存货影响了该资产的账面价值。假如存货未被转移，净资产应该仍会减少 10, 000 英镑，但减少的金额应该会完全体现在存货价值中而现金余额保持不变。然而，集团内移动存货和现金的结果是，存货价值减少 6, 000 英镑，集团现金头寸减少 4, 000 英镑。这反映了集团的外币风险敞口集中在不同资产上的事实。

作为境外经营净投资组成部分的货币性项目

7. 93 报告主体对境外经营的净投资是指报告主体在境外经营净资产中享有的权益金额。（IAS 21 第 8 段）。在下述第 7. 95 段所述情况下，一项应收或应付境外经营的货币性项目，诸如长期贷款和应收款、长期应付款，也许被作

ⓒ 2013 普华永道（PricewaterhouseCoopers）版权所有。

payable to a foreign operation, such as long-term loans and receivables and long-term payables, may be regarded as an extension of, or reduction, in the reporting entity's net investment in that foreign operation. In those situations, it may not be appropriate to include the resulting exchange differences arising on the retranslation of such monetary items in consolidated profit or loss when exchange difference arising on equivalent financing with equity capital would be taken to other comprehensive income on consolidation.

7.94 IAS 21 recognises the above situation and requires exchange differences arising on a monetary item that forms part of a reporting entity's net investment in a foreign operation that is a subsidiary, associate or joint venture to be treated as follows:

- In the separate financial statements of the reporting entity or the individual financial statements of the foreign operation as appropriate, such exchange differences are recognised in the income statement.

- In the financial statements that include the foreign operation and the reporting entity (for example, consolidated financial statements when the foreign operation is a subsidiary), such exchange differences are recognised initially in a separate component of other comprehensive income and recognised in the profit or loss on disposal of the net investment (see further para 7.106).

[IAS 21 para 32].

7.95 The inclusion of long-term loans and receivables as part of the net investment in the foreign operation is only permitted where settlement is neither planned nor likely to occur in the foreseeable future. [IAS 21 para 15]. In other words, the parent must regard them as permanent as equity. For example, a loan to a foreign entity that is repayable on demand may seem to be a short-term item, rather than part of capital. However, if there is demonstrably no intent or expectation to demand repayment (for example, the short-term loan is allowed to be continuously rolled over, whether or not the subsidiary is able to repay it), the loan has the same economic effect as a capital contribution. On the other hand, a long-term loan with a specified maturity (say 10 to 15 years) does not automatically qualify to be treated as being part of the net investment simply

© 2013 PricewaterhouseCoopers LLP. All rights reserved.

为报告主体对该境外经营净投资的延伸或缩减。此种情况下，当产生于等效权益资本融资方式的汇兑差额被计入合并其他综合收益时，将这类货币性项目折算而产生的汇兑差额包括在合并损益中，可能是不适当的。

7.94 IAS 21 确认上述情况并规定作为境外经营子公司、联营或合营企业净投资组成部分的货币性项目所产生的汇兑差额依照如下方式进行处理：

- 在报告主体的单独财务报表或境外经营的个别财务报表中，此类汇兑差额被确认在利润表中是适当的。
- 在同时包括境外经营和报告主体的财务报表（例如，当境外经营为子公司时的合并财务报表）中，此类汇兑差额在初始确认时，作为其他综合收益的单列项，并且在处置该净投资时确认为损益。（参见下述第 7.106 段）。

［IAS 21 第 32 段］。

7.95 只有在可以预见的将来，既未打算也不大可能进行结算的情况下，准许该长期贷款和应收款包括在境外经营净投资中。［IAS 21 第 15 段］。换句话说，母公司必须将其作为等同于权益的永久性投资。例如，向境外主体提供的可随时要求偿还的贷款看起来可能是一个短期项目，并非资本的一部分。但是，如果可以证明管理层没有意图或预期要求偿还（例如，无论子公司是否能够偿还，该短期贷款被允许持续滚动展期），该贷款具有与资本投入相同的经济效应。另一方面，一个具有规定到期时间（比如说 10 年至 15 年）的长期贷款并不只是因为其期限长而自动符合被作为净投资组成部分的条件，除非管理层已表达意愿将于贷款到期之时展期。管理层的任务是以留下审计证据的书面方式，例如董事会会议记录，来明确表达其展期意愿，否则，缺乏管理层的展期意愿，贷款的到期日意味着其在可预见的将来是需要偿还的。

ⓒ 2013 普华永道（PricewaterhouseCoopers）版权所有。

because it is of a long duration, unless management has expressed its intention to renew the note at maturity. The burden is on management to document its intention to renew by auditable evidence, such as board minutes. Otherwise, absent management's intention to renew, the note's maturity date implies that its settlement is planned in the foreseeable future.

7.96 Some may argue that inter-company accounts of a trading nature should qualify for the same treatment as above because, although individual transactions are settled, the account's aggregate balance never drops below a specified minimum. In other words, as a minimum amount is permanently deferred, an appropriate amount of the resulting exchange difference should also be deferred in equity. This treatment is not permitted; the standard prohibits its application to trade receivables and payables. [IAS 21 para 15]. The rationale is that as each individual transaction included in the overall inter-company balance is settled and replaced by a new transaction; settlement is always contemplated and, therefore, exchange gains and losses arising on such active accounts as described above would not qualify for deferral treatment.

7.97 The example below illustrates a number of scenarios setting out the treatment that management is required to follow on consolidation when inter-company loans are made between various members of a group.

Parent A is the reporting entity that has two subsidiaries B and C, which themselves have subsidiaries D and E. The functional currencies of each of the entities are as noted next to the letters designating the entities.

Group structure

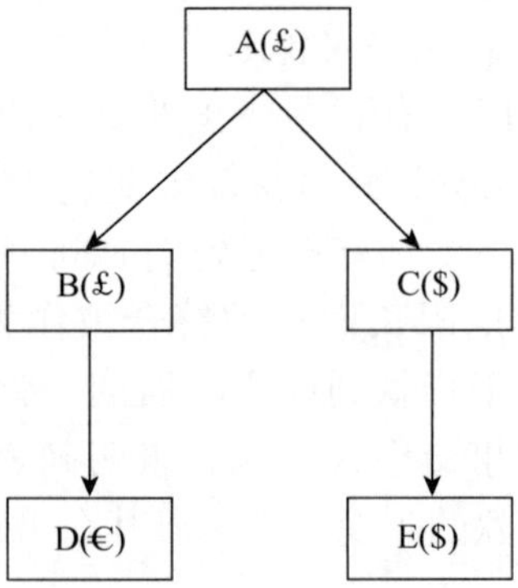

© 2013 PricewaterhouseCoopers LLP. All rights reserved.

7.96　有人可能主张供销性质的公司间账户应当适用同样处理原则，因为尽管单项交易已结算，但该账户的合计余额从未降至某一最低金额以下。换句话说，有个最低金额被永久性递延，由此所产生的汇兑差额也应当在权益中进行递延。这种处理方法是不被准许的；该准则禁止应收账款和应付账款适用该条款。[IAS 21 第 15 段]。其理论基础在于，公司间账户的整体余额中的各单项交易都在不断地被结算并被新发生的交易所更新的过程中，结算始终是一个预期将要发生的事情，所以，产生于如上所述的此类活跃账户的汇兑利得和损失应该不符合递延处理方式。

7.97　下列示例演示了数种情形下，当不同集团成员之间发生公司间贷款时，管理层在合并层面的后续会计处理。

报告主体母公司 A 拥有两个子公司 B 和 C，它们分别拥有子公司 D 和 E。每个主体的功能货币标明在该主体的指定字母代号边。

集团结构

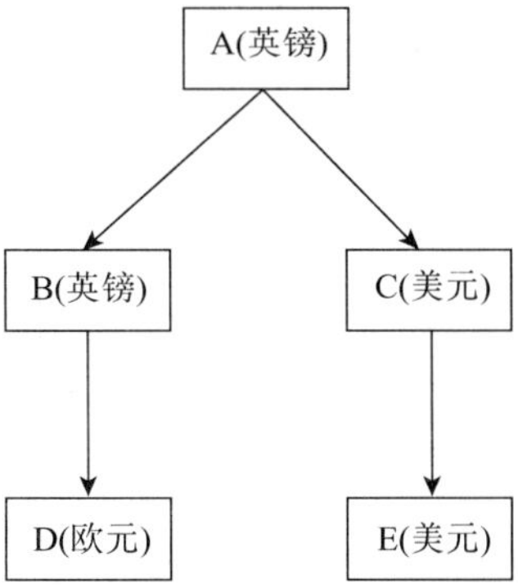

ⓒ 2013 普华永道（PricewaterhouseCoopers）版权所有。

In all the scenarios that follow, loans made between group entities are permanent in nature (that is, settlement is neither planned nor likely to occur).

Scenario 1

Parent A has a loan receivable from or payable to its foreign subsidiary C that is denominated in either sterling or the dollar.

The loan would be regarded as an extension to or a reduction of entity A's net investment in entity C as appropriate. An exchange difference is recognised in entity A's income statement if the loan receivable or payable is denominated in dollars. An exchange difference will be recognised in entity C's income statement if the loan receivable or payable is denominated in sterling. Any exchange difference recognised in either entity's profit or loss is recognised in other comprehensive income on consolidation. The above situation is dealt with in the numerical examples below.

Example – currency loan made by parent A to foreign subsidiary C

Parent A with sterling as its functional currency is preparing its financial statements to 30 September 20X5. It has a loan receivable of US$ 1m from its foreign subsidiary C that has been outstanding for some time. The parent notified the overseas subsidiary at the beginning of the financial year that no repayment of the amount will be requested for the foreseeable future.

The relevant exchange rates are as follows:

	30 September 20X5	30 September 20X4
£1 =	US $ 1.82	US $ 1.45

The following exchange differences will arise in the financial statements of the individual entities if the loan is retranslated at the closing rate:

Foreign subsidiary C

No exchange difference arises in the foreign subsidiary as the loan payable is denominated in its functional currency.

UK parent A

Exchange difference on long-term loan receivable

© 2013 PricewaterhouseCoopers LLP. All rights reserved.

在下述所有示例中，不同集团成员之间的贷款是永久性的（也就是，既未打算也不大可能进行结算）。

情形 1

母公司 A 向境外子公司 C 提供贷款或借入借款，该应收贷款或应付借款以英镑或者美元计价。

该贷款会被作为主体 A 对主体 C 净投资的延伸或缩减是适当的。如果该应收贷款或应付借款以美元计价，汇兑差额被确认在主体 A 的利润表中。如果该应收贷款或应付借款以英镑计价，汇兑差额将被确认在主体 C 的利润表中。于合并层面，A 或 C 任一主体的利润表中确认的汇兑差额将被确认为其他综合收益。上述情况以数字示例列示如下。

示例——母公司 A 向境外子公司 C 提供外币贷款

母公司 A 以英镑作为功能货币，正在编制其截至 20X5 年 9 月 30 日止的财务报表。对其境外子公司 C 的一笔 100 万美元应收贷款久未收回。母公司于财务年度之初告知境外子公司，在可预见的将来不会要求偿还任何款项。

相关汇率如下：

	20X5 年 9 月 30 日	20X4 年 9 月 30 日
1 英镑 =	1. 82 美元	1. 45 美元

如果该笔贷款按期末汇率重新折算，下列汇兑差额将产生于个别主体的财务报表：

境外子公司 C

由于该笔应付借款以其功能货币计价，不会产生汇兑差额。

英国母公司 A

长期应收贷款的汇兑差额

ⓒ 2013 普华永道（PricewaterhouseCoopers）版权所有。

	£
On closing rate – US $ 1m @ 1. 82	549,450
On opening rate – US $ 1m @ 1. 45	689,655
Exchange loss	140,205

In the parent entity's separate financial statement, the loan is regarded as a monetary item and any exchange difference is taken to the profit or loss in accordance with paragraph 7. 94 above. [IAS 21 para 32].

On consolidation, the retranslated long-term loan is regarded as part of the net investment in the foreign subsidiary and, therefore, the related exchange loss is recognised in other comprehensive income and accumulated as a separate component of equity in accordance with paragraph 7. 94 above. [IAS 21 para 32]. There would also be a corresponding exchange gain included in other comprehensive income, arising as part of the retranslation of the net assets (which include the US dollar loan creditor) of the overseas subsidiary under the closing rate/net investment method.

Example – sterling loan made by parent A to overseas subsidiary C

The facts are the same as the above example, except that parent A has a loan receivable from its overseas subsidiary of £200, 000 that has been outstanding for some time. The loan is treated by the parent entity as forming part of its net investment in the overseas subsidiary.

In the financial statements of the individual entities, the following exchange differences will arise if the loan is retranslated at the closing rate.

UK parent A

There is no exchange difference in the parent's financial statements in respect of the loan as it is denominated in sterling.

Subsidiary C

Exchange difference on long-term loan payable	US $
On closing rate – £200, 000 @ 1. 82	364, 000
On opening rate – £200, 000 @ 1. 45	290, 000
Exchange loss	74, 000
Exchange loss translated at the closing rate @ 1. 82	£40,659

© 2013 PricewaterhouseCoopers LLP. All rights reserved.

	英镑
100 万美元按期末汇率 1.82 折算	549,450
100 万美元按期初汇率 1.45 折算	689,655
汇兑损失	140,205

依据上述第 7.94 段，在母公司的单独财务报表中，该笔贷款作为货币性项目，所产生的任何汇兑差额计入损益。[IAS 21 第 32 段]。

在合并层面，由于该长期贷款作为境外经营净投资的组成部分，依据上述第 7.94 段，对其重新折算所产生的相关汇兑损失确认为其他综合收益并作为单列权益项目进行累积。[IAS 21 第 32 段]。用期末汇率/净投资法对境外子公司的净资产（包括该美元应付借款）进行重新折算时，也应该会产生一个相应的汇兑利得，其中包括了由该美元应付借款产生的部分，被包括在合并层面的其他综合收益中。

示例——母公司 A 向境外子公司 C 提供英镑贷款

除下述事项外，承上例。母公司 A 对其境外子公司的一笔 20 万英镑应收贷款久未收回。该贷款被作为母公司向其境外子公司净投资的组成部分。

如果该笔贷款按期末汇率重新折算，个别主体的财务报表中将产生下列汇兑差额。

英国母公司 A

由于该笔贷款以英磅计价，没有汇兑差额。

子公司 C

长期借款的汇兑差额	美元
20 万英镑按期末汇率 1.82 折算	364,000
20 万英镑按期初汇率 1.45 折算	290,000
汇兑损失	74,000
汇兑损失按期末汇率 1.82 折算	40,659 英镑

ⓒ 2013 普华永道（PricewaterhouseCoopers）版权所有。

The exchange loss of US $74,000 on the sterling loan is recognised in the foreign subsidiary C's income statement, because the subsidiary is exposed to the foreign currency risk.

On consolidation, the inter-company loan will cancel out. However, as the long-term loan is regarded as part of the net investment in the subsidiary, the exchange loss of £40,659 is recognised in other comprehensive income and accumulated as a separate component of equity in the consolidated financial statements. There is a corresponding exchange gain included in other comprehensive income arising as part of the retranslation of the net assets of the overseas subsidiary. The effect is that the consolidated income statement will not reflect any exchange difference on the loan, which is consistent with the fact that the loan has no impact on group cash flows, unless the investment is sold.

The two examples above consider the accounting implications when a loan is made by the parent entity to an overseas subsidiary. In the case of a foreign currency upstream loan, for example, a borrowing by a parent entity from its subsidiary in the subsidiary's local currency, the treatment of exchange differences in the consolidated financial statements will depend on whether the loan is regarded as part of the net investment in the subsidiary. If that is the case, the treatment will be the same as identified above. That is, the exchange difference arising on the currency loan's retranslation in the parent's income statement is classified to a separate component of equity in the consolidated financial statements. On the other hand, if the loan is not regarded as part of the net investment, the exchange difference will continue to be recognised in consolidated profit or loss.

Scenario 2

Subsidiary B makes a loan denominated in sterling to subsidiary C ('sister-entity loans')

Subsidiary C recognises an exchange difference in its own income statement. The question is whether the exchange difference can be recognised in other comprehensive income and accumulated as a separate component of equity on

© 2013 PricewaterhouseCoopers LLP. All rights reserved.

因为子公司存在外币风险，该英镑借款产生的汇兑损失 74, 000 美元在境外子公司 C 的利润表中予以确认。

公司间贷款余额将在合并层面抵销。不过，由于该长期贷款作为境外经营净投资的组成部分，汇兑损失 40, 659 英镑在合并财务报表中被确认为其他综合收益并作为单列权益项目进行累积。作为重新折算境外子公司净资产的一部分，有一个相应的汇兑利得被包括在其他综合收益中。其效果是合并利润表不会反映任何该笔贷款产生的汇兑差额，这与除非该净投资被出售，该笔贷款对集团现金流量没有影响的事实相一致。

上述两个示例考虑了母公司向境外子公司提供贷款时的会计影响。当境外子公司反过来向母公司提供贷款的情况下，例如，母公司向子公司借入以子公司当地货币计价的借款，合并财务报表中汇兑差额的处理方法取决于该借款是否被作为母公司对境外子公司净投资的组成部分。如果是的话，处理方法将与上述认定相同。也就是，母公司利润表中由外币借款重新折算所产生的汇兑差额在合并财务报表中被分类为权益科目的单独项目列示。另一方面，如果该借款未被作为净投资的组成部分，汇兑差额将继续确认在合并损益中。

情形 2

子公司 B 向子公司 C 提供一笔以英镑计价的贷款(“兄弟主体间贷款”)

子公司 C 在其自身利润表中确认汇兑差额。问题是该汇兑差额是否在合并层面确认为其他综合收益，并作为单列权益项目进行累积。

ⓒ 2013 普华永道（PricewaterhouseCoopers）版权所有。

consolidation.

IAS 21 has been amended to clarify in paragraph 15A that it is not necessary for the lender or the borrower to have the net investment in the foreign operation for the exchange differences on translation of the monetary item to be classified within entity. The entity that has the monetary item receivable from or payable to a foreign operation may be any member of group.

7.98 The above examples deal with situations where a monetary item forming part of the net investment was denominated in the functional currency of either the reporting entity or the foreign operation. The question then arises as to whether a similar treatment is permissible in circumstances where a monetary item forming part of the net investment in a foreign operation is denominated in a currency that is different from the functional currency of either the reporting entity or the foreign operation.

7.99 Under IAS 21, a monetary item that meets the criteria to be part of an entity's net investment in a foreign operation is similar to an equity investment in a foreign operation. Hence, the accounting treatment in the consolidated financial statements does not depend on the currency in which the monetary item is denominated. Paragraph 33 of IAS 21 requires exchange differences on translation of such a monetary item to be recognised in other comprehensive income in the consolidated financial statements, irrespective of the currency of the monetary item.

7.99.1 Consider the situation in the group structure set out in paragraph 7.97 above where parent A, whose functional currency is the pound sterling, makes a loan denominated in euros to subsidiary C, whose functional currency is the US dollar. If the euro loan meets the criteria to be regarded by entity A as part of its net investment in entity C, the exchange differences that arise from retranslating the loan receivable in sterling in entity A's income statement and the loan payable in dollars in entity C's income statement are recognised in other comprehensive income in the financial statements that include the foreign operation and the reporting entity (that is, entity A's consolidated financial statements). [IAS 21 para 33].

© 2013 PricewaterhouseCoopers LLP. All rights reserved.

IAS 21 已被修改并在第 15A 段中澄清，贷款方或借款方是否拥有该境外经营净投资不是货币性项目汇兑差额能否在主体内进行分类的必要条件。报告主体可以是任何向境外经营提供应收或应付货币性项目的集团成员。

7.98 作为净投资的组成部分，上述示例中涉及的是当货币性项目以报告主体或该境外经营的功能货币来计价的情况。由此引发的问题是，当作为境外经营净投资组成部分的货币性项目以既不同于报告主体的功能货币、又不同于境外经营的功能货币来计价的情况下，类似的处理方法是否被准许。

7.99 根据 IAS 21，判断一个货币性项目是否符合报告主体对境外经营净投资的组成部分，是看其是否类似于在境外经营中的权益性投资。因此，在合并财务报表中的会计处理并不取决于该货币性项目以何种货币计价。IAS 21 第 33 段规定，此类货币性项目折算产生的汇兑差额确认为合并财务报表中的其他综合收益，与该货币性项目的计价货币无关。

7.99.1 考虑一下上述第 7.97 段所述的集团结构中的情况——在以英镑为功能货币的母公司 A 向以美元为功能货币的子公司 C 提供一笔欧元贷款的情况下，如果该欧元贷款符合报告主体 A 对主体 C 净投资的组成部分，那么由于折算主体 A 的应收贷款和主体 C 的应付借款而产生且分别确认于各自利润表中的汇兑差额在同时包括境外经营及报告主体的财务报表（也就是主体 A 的合并财务报表）中确认为其他综合收益。[IAS 21 第 33 段]。

ⓒ 2013 普华永道（PricewaterhouseCoopers）版权所有。

7.100 Another issue that might arise is the appropriate treatment to be adopted in the year in which the parent decides to designate any long-term loans and receivables as part of its net investment in the foreign operation. Consider the first example in scenario 1 above where the long-term US dollar loan made by parent A was designated as being part of its net investment in the foreign subsidiary C from the beginning of the accounting period. If the parent did this part way through the financial year ended 30 September 20X5, say, at 31 March 20X5, the parent recognises any exchange difference arising in profit or loss up to that date and reclassifies any exchange difference that arises subsequently following the designation to the separate component in other comprehensive income in the consolidated financial statements.

7.101 Although not dealt with in the standard, the designation of an inter-company loan as part of the net investment in a foreign operation is periodically reassessed. This is because management's expectations and intent may change due to a change in circumstances. Such changes in circumstances are carefully evaluated to determine that management's previous assertions for not requiring repayment remain valid. For example, the change in circumstances may be such that it could not have been anticipated at the time of initial designation or the change in circumstances could be outside management's control.

7.102 Where, as a result of a change in circumstance, a previously designated 'net investment' loan is intended to be settled, the loan is de-designated. As the loan is no longer regarded as part of the net investment, a partial disposal of the net investment may have occurred and reclassification of cumulative translation adjustment may be required. See from paragraph 7.106 onwards for discussion of partial disposals.

7.102.1 There is no explicit guidance in IAS 21 about the timing of reclassification in the circumstances described in the previous paragraph. Does it occur when the loan is no longer considered to form part of the net investment in the foreign operation, or when the loan is actually repaid? Either approach may be adopted as an accounting policy choice. The selected policy should be applied consistently to all of the entity's 'net investment' loans and to all of its investments in foreign operations.

© 2013 PricewaterhouseCoopers LLP. All rights reserved.

7.100　另一个可能出现的问题是，当母公司决定指定任何长期贷款和应收款作为其境外经营净投资组成部分的当年度所应采用的适当的会计处理方法。考虑一下上述情形1中的第一个示例——在母公司A提供的长期美元贷款自会计期间的期初就被指定为其对境外子公司C净投资的组成部分的情况下，如果母公司对该美元贷款的指定发生在截至20X5年9月30日止的财务年度期间中，比如说，于20X5年3月31日，那么母公司在利润表中对产生的汇兑损益确认至该指定日止，并将产生于该指定日之后的汇兑差额在合并财务报表中重分类至其他综合收益的单列项目。

7.101　虽然准则中未涉及，管理层需要定期对其所指定的作为境外经营净投资组成部分的公司间贷款进行评价。这是因为管理层的预期和意图可能因情况变化而改变。此类情况变化需要仔细评价，以确定管理层先前对于不要求偿还的判定依然有效。例如，情况变化可能是最初指定时不可预见或者可能是管理层控制范围以外的。

7.102　在情况发生变化的结果导致原先被指定为“净投资”的贷款将被结算的情况下，对该贷款的指定被终止。由于该贷款不再作为净投资的组成部分，可能已造成对净投资的部分处置，因而可能需要对累计折算差额进行重分类调整。参见自第7.106段起有关部分处置的讨论。

7.102.1　对于上段所述情况何时进行重分类调整，IAS 21中没有明确的指引。发生在贷款不再被作为境外经营净投资组成部分之时？或者发生在该贷款实际被偿还之时？两种方法可任选一种，作为会计政策的选择。所选会计政策应当一致性地应用于主体所有的“净投资”贷款及其所有的境外经营。

ⓒ 2013 普华永道（PricewaterhouseCoopers）版权所有。

Inter-entity dividends

7.103 Where a foreign subsidiary pays a dividend to its parent entity, the dividend is charged directly to equity in its financial statements, and as the dividend is paid in the functional currency of the foreign subsidiary no exchange difference arises. However, if the dividends are payable in a currency that is different from the subsidiary's functional currency, exchange rate fluctuations between the dividend being recognised as an asset and being paid will produce foreign exchange gains or losses impacting profit or loss.

7.104 In the parent entity's financial statements, the dividend is translated at the rate in effect upon declaration (that is, the transaction date). An exchange gain or loss will arise if the rate of exchange moves between the date of declaration and the payment date. This exchange difference is reported in the parent's income statement as a normal inter-company transaction exchange gain or loss that is also reported in the consolidated financial statements. Consider the following example:

Example – Treatment of foreign exchange gains or losses on inter-entity dividends

A subsidiary with a dollar functional currency declared a dividend of $100,000 to its euro functional currency parent on 31 August 20X5 for the year ended 31 December 20X5. The dividend was appropriately authorised and recognised by the subsidiary as a liability at 31 August 20X5. The parent prepares consolidated financial statements for the year ended 31 December 20X5 in its presentation currency of euros. The following exchange rates are relevant:

31 August 20X5	$1.50 = €1
31 December 20X5	$1.75 = €1
15 January 20X6	$1.80 = €1

Dividend paid on 15 January 20X6

The dividend remains outstanding at the balance sheet date. The dividend is recorded in the subsidiary's and parent's separate and consolidated financial statements as follows:

© 2013 PricewaterhouseCoopers LLP. All rights reserved.

主体间股利

7.103　在境外子公司向其母公司主体支付股利的情况下，股利直接记入其财务报表中的权益，且由于该股利是以境外子公司的功能货币支付的，不产生汇兑差额。然而，如果应付股利以不同于子公司的功能货币的货币计价，自该股利被确认为一项资产至其完成支付的期间，汇率的变动将会产生影响损益的汇兑利得或损失。

7.104　在母公司主体的财务报表中，股利以宣告日（也就是交易日）的实际汇率折算。如果汇率在宣告日与付款日之间发生变动，将会产生汇兑利得或损失。汇兑差额作为正常的公司间交易的汇兑利得或损失记入母公司的利润表，也记入合并财务报表。考虑下面的示例：

示例——主体间股利的汇兑损益的处理

以美元为功能货币的子公司于20X5年8月31日宣布，在截至20X5年12月31日止年度，向其以欧元为功能货币的母公司派发股利100,000美元。该股利经适当授权，并于20X5年8月31日由子公司确认为负债。母公司以欧元作为其列报货币编制截至20X5年12月31日止年度的合并财务报表。以下为相关汇率：

20X5年8月31日	1.50美元=1英镑
20X5年12月31日	1.75美元=1英镑
20X6年1月15日	1.80美元=1英镑

股利于20X6年1月15日支付

该股利于资产负债表日尚未支付。股利在子公司的单独财务报表中、母公司的单独及合并财务报表中记录如下：

ⓒ 2013 普华永道（PricewaterhouseCoopers）版权所有。

In subsidiary's balance sheet (as translated for consolidation)

	€
Dividend payable – $ 100,000 @ 1.75	57,142

In parent's income statement

Initially recorded at rate when dividend is declared – $ 100,000 @ 1.5 (transaction date)	66,667
Exchange loss on receivable recognised in the income statement	(9,525)
In parent's balance sheet – Dividend receivable at year end rate – $ 100,000 @ 1.75	57,142

In consolidated income statement

In the consolidated financial statements the dividend receivable of € 66,667 is reclassified to consolidated retained earnings and offsets the dividend payable in the subsidiary's retained earnings that is translated at the year end rate @ 1.75 = € 57,142. The difference of € 9,525 (€ 66,667 – € 57,142) comprises a loss recorded in the parent's income statement and no further exchange difference arises. The inter-entity receivable and payable cancel out.

Some may argue that the exchange difference of € 9,525 included in the parent's income statement should be removed from consolidated income and reclassified to equity as it relates to dividends that are initially charged to equity. We believe that this treatment is not appropriate, as the exchange difference arises on a monetary asset and would affect group cash flows when it is settled. Such an exchange difference should, therefore, remain in consolidated income.

7.105 Given that exchange differences can arise on any transaction where the settlement date is different from the date when the transaction is recorded, it may be appropriate to ensure that inter-entity dividends are paid on the same date as they are declared as liabilities, particularly where it is likely that an exchange loss will arise. This may not always be possible, so it is not uncommon for a parent entity to mitigate exchange differences arising by taking out appropriate forward contracts so as to hedge the future remittance. Hedge accounting for foreign currency items

© 2013 PricewaterhouseCoopers LLP. All rights reserved.

在子公司的资产负债表中（与合并层面所作的折算相同）

	欧元
应付股利——10 万美元按 1.75 折算	57,142

在母公司的利润表中

按照股利宣告时的汇率进行初始入账——10 万美元按 1.5 折算（交易日）	66,667
应收款的汇兑损失在利润表中进行确认	(9,525)
在母公司的资产负债表中——按年末汇率计算的应收股利——10 万美元按 1.75 折算	57,142

在合并利润表中

在合并财务报表中，应收股利 66,667 英镑被重分类至合并留存收益，并与按年底汇率（1.75）折算为 57,142 英镑的子公司留存收益中的应付股利相抵消。差额 9,525 英镑（66,667 英镑 - 57,142 英镑）构成记入母公司利润表的损失，不再进一步产生汇兑差额。主体间的应收款和应付款互相抵消。

有人可能主张应当将包括在母公司利润表中的汇兑差额 9,525 英镑从合并收益中移出并重分类至权益，因为其与初始被记入权益的股利相关。我们认为这一处理方法是不合适的，因为汇兑差额产生于货币性资产，当其被结算时应该会影响到集团的现金流量。因此，此类汇兑差额应当留在合并收益中。

7.105　考虑到在结算日不同于交易入账日的情况下，任何交易均会产生这样的汇兑差额，适当的作法可能是确保主体间股利在其宣告日即被支付，特别在有可能产生汇兑损失的情况下。这或许并不总是可行的，因而母公司主体通过取得适当的远期合同，以套期未来的股利汇款，从而减少产生的汇兑差额并不少见。IAS 39 中论及外币项目套期会计。套期会计在《国际财务报告准则实务指引——金融工具系列》第十章中进行阐述。

ⓒ 2013 普华永道（PricewaterhouseCoopers）版权所有。

is dealt with in IAS 39. Hedge accounting is considered in chapter 10 of IFRS Manual of Accounting – Financial Instruments.

Disposal or partial disposal of a foreign operation

7.106 As discussed in paragraph 7.77, the cumulative amount of exchange differences recognised in other comprehensive income (cumulative translation adjustment, or CTA) is carried forward as a separate component of equity until there is a disposal of the foreign operation. On the foreign operation's disposal, such exchange differences are recognised in profit or loss (that is, reclassified) when the gain or loss on disposal is recognised. [IAS 21 para 48]. Disposal may occur either through sale, liquidation, repayment of share capital or a quasi-equity loan, or abandonment of all, or part of, the entity.

7.106.1 When an entity loses control of a subsidiary that includes a foreign operation this is a disposal that triggers reclassification of the entire amount of CTA that has been recorded in equity attributable to the parent entity, even if the entity retains an interest in that former subsidiary. [IAS 21 para 48, 48A]. This applies, for example, when 80% of a 100% subsidiary is sold and a 20% interest in an associate is retained. The entire amount of CTA in relation to that subsidiary is reclassified to profit or loss. In the case where a foreign operation is partially owned (that is, where a non-controlling interest exists) the amount of the CTA that has been allocated to the non-controlling interest is derecognised, but is not transferred to profit or loss. [IAS 21 para 48B]. De-recognition of the non-controlling interest that includes the non-controlling interest's share of CTA will form part of the journal to calculate the gain or loss on disposal of the foreign operation.

7.106.2 The principle of full reclassification also applies to the loss of joint control or significant influence over a jointly controlled entity or an associate. All CTA that has been accumulated in equity in relation to that jointly controlled entity or associate is reclassified to profit or loss when joint control or significant influence is lost. [IAS 21 para 48A].

7.107 On a partial disposal that does not involve loss of control of a subsidiary that includes a foreign operation, the entity re-attributes the proportionate share of

© 2013 PricewaterhouseCoopers LLP. All rights reserved.

境外经营的处置或部分处置

7.106　如第7.77段所讨论的，在其他综合收益中所确认的汇兑差额的累积金额（累计折算调整或CTA），作为单列权益项目结转后期，直至该境外经营被处置时为止。当该境外经营被处置，确认处置利得或损失时，此类汇兑差额被确认为损益（也就是，被重分类）。[IAS 21第48段]。处置可以通过出售、清算、返还股本或准权益贷款，或者放弃全部或部分权益而发生。

7.106.1　某一含有境外经营的子公司，当主体失去对其的控制权时，即使主体仍保留在该子公司中的权益，这是一个引发已被记录在可归属于母公司主体权益中的累计折算调整的全部金额被重分类的处置。[IAS 21第48段、第48A段]。这适用于，例如，当出售一个全资子公司80%的权益并以联营形式保留20%权益的时候。有关该子公司的全部累计折算调整金额被重分类至损益。对于在境外经营为非全资（也就是，当存在非控制性权益的情况）的情况下，已归属于非控制性权益的累计折算调整金额被终止确认，而不是转为损益。[IAS 21第48B段]。对于含有非控制性权益份额累计折算调整的非控制性权益的终止确认，将构成计算处置境外经营利得或损失的会计分录的一部分。

7.106.2　完全重分类原则也适用于对共同控制主体失去共同控制权或对联营企业丧失重大影响之时。当失去共同控制权或重大影响时，已累积在权益中的与共同控制主体或联营企业相关的累计折算调整被重分类至损益。[IAS 21第48A段]。

7.107　当不涉及丧失控制权，部分处置含有境外经营的子公司时，主体将该境外经营中相应比例的累计折算调整重新归属至非控制性权益。[IAS 21第

ⓒ 2013 普华永道（PricewaterhouseCoopers）版权所有。

the CTA to the non-controlling interests in that foreign operation. [IAS 21 para 48C].

7.107.1 On the partial disposal of an interest in a jointly controlled entity or an associate, where joint control or significant influence are not lost, a proportionate amount of CTA is reclassified to profit or loss. [IAS 21 para 48C].

7.107.2 A write-down of the carrying amount of a foreign operation does not constitute a partial disposal. No part of the deferred foreign exchange gain or loss is recognised in profit or loss at the time of a write-down. [IAS 21 para 49]. Where the write-down arises from an impairment assessment as a result of a planned sale or liquidation (for example, where the foreign subsidiary is treated as a disposal group in accordance with IFRS 5 the writedown is also not treated as a partial disposal. [IFRS 5 BC 37, 38]. Therefore, any exchange difference attributable to that write down is not recognised in profit or loss. Reclassification will occur when the foreign operation is sold.

7.107.3 The cessation of hedge accounting of a net investment as the hedge no longer meets the criteria for the hedge accounting in IAS 39 is not a disposal. Therefore, the effective portion of the hedge as well as the related CTA previously recognised in other comprehensive income remain in other comprehensive income until the disposal, or partial disposal, of the foreign operation.

7.107.4 The conversion of a 'net investment' loan to an equity instrument as defined in IAS 32 does not result in reclassification. The reason for this is that the conversion of the loan is the swapping of the legal form of an investment from a debt instrument to an equity instrument so no disposal has occurred. No further exchange differences will arise on the equity investment in the parent's separate financial statements, as it is now a non-monetary item. (However, exchange differences would continue to arise on the net assets of the foreign operation.) The redenomination of a 'net investment' loan into a different currency also does not constitute a disposal or partial disposal of the foreign operation. It does not change the parent's net investment in the foreign operation, there is no cash movement therefore in substance there has been no disposal. Therefore, no gains or losses are reclassified from equity to profit or loss.

© 2013 PricewaterhouseCoopers LLP. All rights reserved.

48C 段]。

7.107.1 在未丧失共同控制权或重要影响的情况下，当部分处置共同控制主体或联营企业中的权益时，相应比例的累计折算调整被重分类至损益。[IAS 21 第 48C 段]。

7.107.2 对境外经营账面价值的减记，不构成部分处置。当减记发生时，无需将部分递延汇兑利得或损失确认为损益。[IAS 21 第 49 段]。在减记产生于因有计划出售或清算而进行减值测试的情况下（例如，在国外子公司根据 IFRS 5 被作为处置组的情况下），减记也不被作为部分处置。[IFRS 5 BC 第 37 段、第 38 段]。因此，可归属于该减记资产的任何汇兑差额不被确认为损益。重分类将发生在该境外经营被出售之时。

7.107.3 因套期不再符合 IAS 39 中对于套期会计处理之标准而停止对净投资的套期会计处理不是一项处置。因此，套期的有效部分以及原先在其他综合收益中所确认的相关累计折算调整，在处置或部分处置境该外经营之前，留在其他综合收益中。

7.107.4 将“净投资”贷款转换成 IAS 32 所定义的权益工具不会导致重分类。原因是，贷款的转换是从债务工具到权益工具的法律形式的互换，因而未发生过处置。在母公司的单独财务报表中，权益投资不会进一步产生汇兑差额，因为它现在是非货币性项目（然而，境外经营净资产应该会继续产生汇兑差额）。“净投资”贷款以另一种货币单位重新计价，也不构成对境外经营的处置或部分处置。它未改变母公司在境外经营中的净投资，没有现金流的变动，因而实质上没有发生过处置。所以，无需将利得或损失由权益重分类至损益。

ⓒ 2013 普华永道（PricewaterhouseCoopers）版权所有。

7.107.5 A partial disposal is areduction in an entity's 'ownership interest' in a foreign operation, other than loss of control, significant influence or joint control (see paras 7.106.1, 7.107.1). [IAS 21 para 48D]. Where a subsidiary that is a foreign operation repays a quasi-equity loan or repays/returns share capital but there is no change in the parent's proportionate percentage shareholding there is an accounting policy choice regarding whether the CTA should be reclassified depending on how 'ownership interest' in IAS 21 is interpreted.

Option 1 – No disposal of interest in subsidiary

Since the parent continues to own the same percentage of the subsidiary, and continues to control the foreign operation, there has been no change in its proportionate 'ownership interest' and hence no disposal or partial disposal under paragraphs 48D and 49 of IAS 21. Under this view 'ownership interest' refers only to the proportionate interest. The CTA should not, therefore, be reclassified.

Option 2 – Disposal of interest in subsidiary

The transaction is a partial disposal under paragraph 49 of IAS 21, as there has been a reduction in the parent's absolute ownership interest. Under this view, in addition to a proportionate change in ownership being a partial disposal, 'ownership interest' can also be interpreted as a change in the absolute interest held in a net investment. A *pro rata* share of the CTA should be reclassified.

Entities should make an accounting policy choice between these two methods and apply this policy consistently.

7.107.6 The receipt of a dividend from a foreign operation may only be considered a disposal or partial disposal when it is in substance a repayment/return of capital or liquidation and the parent entity applies the policy of treating such events as partial disposals (see para 7.107.5 and example 3 in para 7.107.7 below). [IAS 21 para 48D].

7.107.7 The rules on disposals and partial disposals and their effect on CTA can be summarised in the following table:

© 2013 PricewaterhouseCoopers LLP. All rights reserved.

7.107.5　部分处置是指除失去控制、重大影响或共同控制之外，主体在境外经营中所有权权益的减少（参见第 7.106.1 段及第 7.107.1 段）。［IAS 21 第 48D 段］。在境外经营子公司偿还准权益贷款或返还股本，而母公司相应持股比例无变化的情况下，根据 IAS 21 对“所有权权益”的解释，关于累计折算调整是否应当被重分类是一个会计政策的选择。

选择 1——所持有的子公司权益未被处置

根据 IAS 21 第 48D 段和第 49 段，因为母公司继续对子公司拥有相同的权益比例，并继续控制该境外经营，其“所有权权益”比例未发生过改变，故未发生处置或部分处置。在此观点下，“所有权权益”仅指权益比例，所以累计折算调整不应当被重分类。

选择 2——处置了所持有的子公司权益

根据 IAS 21 第 49 段，因为母公司所有权权益的绝对额已被减少，该交易为部分处置。根据这一观点，部分处置除了指所有权权益比例的变动之外，“所有权权益”也可以解释为所持净投资权益的绝对额的变动。累计折算调整应当按照比例进行重分类。

主体应当在这两种方法之间作出会计政策选择，并前后一贯地执行这一政策。

7.107.6　只有当事实上构成资本偿还/返还或者清算，且母公司选择将此类事件适用部分处置的会计政策（参见下述第 7.107.5 段和第 7.107.6 段中示例 3）时，从境外经营中收到的股利才有可能被作为处置或部分处置。［IAS 21 第 48D 段］。

7.107.7　处置和部分处置的规则及其对累计折算调整的影响可以被汇总如下表所示：

ⓒ 2013 普华永道（PricewaterhouseCoopers）版权所有。

Event	Disposal or partial disposal	Effect on CTA
Subsidiary to Subsidiary (change in non-controlling interest)	Partial disposal	Reattribute proportionate share of CTA to NCI
Subsidiary to JV or Associate (loss of control)	Disposal	All CTA reclassified to profit or loss
Subsidiary to Investment (loss of control)	Disposal	All CTA reclassified to profit or loss
Associate to Associate (reduction in ownership percentage)	Partial disposal	Proportionate share of CTA reclassified to profit or loss
Associate or JV to Investment	Disposal	All CTA reclassified to profit or loss
Write down of carrying amount of foreign operation	Neither	None
Cessation of hedge accounting for a net investment	Neither	None
Conversion of 'net investment' loan to equity instrument	Neither	None
Repayment of quasi equity loan	Accounting policy choice	Depends on policy choice
Dividend	Depends on substance and policy choice	If in substance the dividend payment is a return of capital or liquidation there is an accounting policy choice – disposal or non disposal. If in substance it is not a return of capital or liquidation, – it is not a disposal/partial disposal.

© 2013 PricewaterhouseCoopers LLP. All rights reserved.

事件	处置或部分处置	对累计折算调整的影响
子公司变为子公司（非控制性权益的变化）	部分处置	重新归属非控制性权益中累计折算调整的相应比例
子公司变为合营或联营（丧失控制权）	处置	所有累计折算调整被重分类至损益
子公司变为投资（丧失控制权）	处置	所有累计折算调整被重分类至损益
联营变为联营（减少所有权比例）	部分处置	相应比例的累计折算调整被重分类至损益
联营或合营变为投资	处置	所有累计折算调整被重分类至损益
减记境外经营的账面价值	两者皆不需要	无
停止对净投资的套期会计处理	两者皆不需要	无
“净投资”贷款转换为权益工具	两者皆不需要	无
偿还准权益贷款	会计政策选择	取决于政策的选择
股利	取决于实质和政策选择	如果股利分配实质上是资本返还或清算，则存在会计政策的选择——处置或不处置。 如果实质上不是资本返还或清算，则不是处置或部分处置。

© 2013 普华永道（PricewaterhouseCoopers）版权所有。

Example 1 – Partial disposal of an associate

An investor owns 40% of the share capital of an entity. It has significant influence over the entity and accounts for the investment as an associate using equity accounting. The associate is a foreign operation. The investor sells half of its total shareholding, retaining a 20% investment. It continues to have significant influence and to account for the investment as an associate.

How much, if any, CTA is reclassified to profit or loss?

The reduction in the investor's ownership interest is a partial disposal per paragraph 48D of IAS 21. Half of the investment in associate has been disposed of, therefore 50% of the CTA relating to the foreign associate is reclassified to profit or loss [IAS 21 para 48C].

Example 2 – Partial disposal of a subsidiary while control is retained

A parent owns 100% of a subsidiary. The subsidiary is a foreign operation. The parent sells 30% of its shareholding, retaining a 70% shareholding and control.

How much, if any, CTA should be reattributed to the non-controlling interest?

The reduction in the parent's ownership interest is a partial disposal per paragraph 48D of IAS 21. 30% of the subsidiary has been disposed of, therefore 30% of CTA should be re-attributed to the new non-controlling interest. This transfer is accounted for in the statement of changes in equity and is not presented in the performance statements. None of the CTA is reclassified to the income statement. [IAS 21 para 48C].

Example 3 – Repayment of a quasi equity loan

A parent owns 100% of a subsidiary. The subsidiary is a foreign operation. The subsidiary repays a quasi-equity loan by paying cash equal to 10% of its net assets to its parent. Prior to the transaction there had been no intention of repaying the quasi-equity loan. After the transaction the parent continues to own 100% of the subsidiary.

© 2013 PricewaterhouseCoopers LLP. All rights reserved.

示例1——对联营企业的部分处置

一位投资者拥有主体40%的股本。投资者对该主体具有重大影响并将该投资作为联营企业按权益法核算。该联营企业是一个境外经营。投资者出售其全部持股的一半，保留20%的投资。投资者继续具有重大影响，仍将该投资作为联营企业核算。

如果有的话，应有多少的累计折算调整被重分类至损益？

根据IAS 21第48D段，投资者减少其所有权权益为部分处置。由于一半的联营企业投资已被处置，所以与该境外联营企业相关的累计折算调整的50%被重分类至损益［IAS 21第48C段］。

示例2——保留控制权情况下对子公司的部分处置

一个母公司拥有的全资子公司。该子公司为境外经营。母公司出售其30%的股权，保留70%的股权和控制权。

如果有的话，应当有多少的累计折算调整被重新归属于非控制性权益？

根据IAS 21第48D段，母公司所有权权益的减少为部分处置。子公司30%的股权已被处置，因而30%的累计折算调整应当被重新归属于非控制性权益。这一转让在权益变动表中核算，不在业绩报表中列报。无任何累计折算调整被重分类至利润表。［IAS 21第48C段］。

示例3——偿还准权益贷款

一个母公司拥有的全资子公司。该子公司为境外经营。子公司通过向其母公司支付等同于10%净资产的现金，偿还一笔准权益贷款。该笔交易之前，未曾有过偿还准权益贷款的意图。交易之后，母公司继续拥有子公司100%的股权。

© 2013 普华永道（PricewaterhouseCoopers）版权所有。

How much, if any, CTA is reclassified to profit or loss?

There are two ways that this transaction might be analysed (para 7.107.5).

Option 1 – No disposal of interest in subsidiary

Since there has been no change in the parent's proportionate 'ownership interest' there is no disposal or partial disposal under paragraphs 48D and 49 of IAS 21. CTA should not, therefore, be reclassified.

Option 2 – Disposal of interest in subsidiary

The transaction is a partial disposal under paragraph 49 of IAS 21, as there has been a 10% reduction in the parent's absolute ownership interest. A pro rata share (10%) of CTA should be reclassified.

The above options would equally apply to a return of capital/repayment of share capital in similar circumstances.

Entities should make an accounting policy choice between these views and apply this policy consistently.

Example 4 – Reclassification of cumulative exchange differences due to a group restructuring

In a group restructuring, a foreign operation is transferred from one intermediate holding entity to another. The group continues to hold a 100% interest in that foreign operation. No third parties are involved with the group restructuring.

Are the cumulative exchange differences reclassified in the group's consolidated financial statements?

The key question is whether the restructuring results in an economic change from the group's perspective that constitutes a partial or full disposal. The foreign operation continues to be part of the consolidated group and the restructuring is not a disposal event from the group's perspective.

However, if the intermediate holding entity that disposes of the foreign operation prepares consolidated financial statements under IFRS, the

© 2013 PricewaterhouseCoopers LLP. All rights reserved.

如果有的话，应有多少的累计折算调整被重分类至损益?

这一交易可能有两种分析方法（第7.107.5段）。

选择1——所持有的子公司权益未被处置

根据IAS 21第48D段和第49段，由于母公司的“所有权权益”比例未曾发生改变，所以没有发生处置或部分处置。因此，累计折算调整不应当被重分类。

选择2——处置了所持有的子公司权益

根据IAS 21第49段，该交易为部分处置，因为母公司所持所有权权益的绝对额已被减少10%。相应比例（10%）的累计折算调整应当被重分类。

上述选择应该会同等地适用于类似情况下的资本返还/股本偿还。

主体应当在这两种观点之间作出会计政策的选择，并前后一贯地执行这一政策。

示例4——由于集团重组造成累计汇兑差额的重分类

集团重组中，一个中间控股主体将境外经营转移给另一个中间控股主体。集团继续持有该境外经营100%的权益。集团重组未涉及第三方。

在集团合并财务报表中的累计汇兑差额被重分类吗?

关键问题是，从集团角度来看，重组是否导致了经济变化从而构成部分或全部处置。从集团角度来看，该境外经营仍然是合并层面集团的一部分，重组不是一个处置事件。

然而，如果由编制国际财务报告准则项下合并财务报表的中间控股主体处置境外经营，在该中间报表层面产生并在权益中递延的累计折算调整

ⓒ 2013 普华永道（PricewaterhouseCoopers）版权所有。

cumulative translation adjustments deferred in equity (if any) that arise at that intermediate reporting level are reclassified to profit or loss.

7.107.8 The tracking of cumulative exchange differences can be onerous. For a parent with more than one foreign operation, it could be tempting to aggregate these exchange differences related to all the net investments in one currency together, with the reclassification of these exchange differences on the disposal (or partial disposal) of some of those foreign operations being calculated proportionately based on the whole investments portfolio. However, IAS 21 requires reclassification whenever there is a disposal, or partial disposal, of a foreign operation, so the cumulative translation adjustments are required to be tracked on an individual net investment basis.

Hedging a net investment

7.108 A net investment in a foreign operation is defined as '*the amount of the reporting entity's interest in the net assets of that operation*'. [IAS 21 para 8]. Management may decide to hedge against the effects of changes in exchange rates in the entity's net investment in a foreign operation. This may be done by taking out a foreign currency borrowing or a forward contract to hedge the net investment. Hedging a net investment in a foreign operation can only be carried out at the consolidation level, because the net assets of the foreign operation are reported in the reporting entity's consolidated financial statements. However, IAS 21 does not apply to hedge accounting for foreign currency items including the hedging of a net investment in a foreign operation. IAS 39 and IFRIC 16 apply to hedge accounting. Under IAS 39, the hedging documentation and criteria set out in paragraph 88 of IAS 39 must be met, and any exchange differences recognised in equity through other comprehensive income relating to the foreign operation and the related borrowing are recognised in profit or loss on disposal of the foreign operation. IFRIC 16 gives further detailed guidance on hedges of net investments. Hedging of net investments is addressed in greater detail in chapter 10 of IFRS Manual of Accounting – Financial Instruments.

7.108.1 Where a reporting entity has a foreign currency borrowing that is designated as a hedge of its net investment in a foreign operation and all the conditions in IAS 39 and IFRIC 16 are met, the exchange gain or loss on the

© 2013 PricewaterhouseCoopers LLP. All rights reserved.

（如果有的话）被重分类至损益。

7.107.8 追踪累计汇兑差额可能是繁琐的。对于拥有一个以上境外经营的母公司，可能很想将这些与所有净投资相关的汇兑差额汇总起来以一种货币计价，并按相对于整个投资组合的比例计算由处置（或部分处置）某些境外经营而引起的重分类。然而，无论何时只要处置或部分处置境外经营，IAS 21 要求重分类，所以需要以个别净投资为基础对累计折算调整进行追踪。

对净投资的套期

7.108 境外经营净投资被定义为“*报告主体在该经营的净资产中享有的权益金额*”。[IAS 21 第 8 段]。管理层可能决定用套期来对冲由于汇率变动对主体的境外经营净投资造成的影响。这可以通过借入外币借款，或者购买远期合同实现对净投资的套期。对境外经营净投资的套期只能在合并层面进行，因为境外经营净资产是在报告主体的合并财务报表中被报告的。然而，IAS 21 并不适用对外币项目的套期会计处理，包括对境外经营净投资的套期。IAS 39 及 IFRIC 16 适用于套期会计处理。根据 IAS 39，必须满足 IAS 39 第 88 段所规定的形成正式书面套期文件和标准，并且通过其他综合收益确认在权益中的与该境外经营和相关借款相关的任何汇兑差额，在该境外经营被处置时确认为损益。IFRIC 16 对于净投资的套期给予更为详尽的指引。对净投资的套期在《国际财务报告准则实务指引——金融工具系列》第十章中有非常详尽的论述。

7.108.1 在报告主体有一笔被指定为对其境外经营净投资进行套期的外币借款，且满足 IAS 39 和 IFRIC 16 所有条件的情况下，报告主体的单独利润表中所报告的外币借款的汇兑利得或损失，在报告主体的合并财务报表中被重分

ⓒ 2013 普华永道（PricewaterhouseCoopers）版权所有。

foreign currency borrowing reported in the reporting entity's separate income statement is reclassified to other comprehensive income in the reporting entity's consolidated financial statements.

7.108.2 IAS 27 states that in a parent's separate financial statements, investments in subsidiaries, jointly controlled entities and associates that are included in the consolidated financial statements are carried at cost or accounted for in accordance with IAS 39. This means that the equity investment can either be carried at cost less impairment, designated as 'available for sale' or designated as 'at fair value through profit or loss' (if permitted by IAS 39). IAS 27 requires the same accounting to be applied for each category of investment. A question arises as to whether a foreign currency borrowing can be designated as a hedge of the entity's foreign equity investment in its separate financial statements where the foreign equity investment is recorded at cost. IAS 39's rules on net investment hedging apply only to consolidated financial statements. However, we believe that the reporting entity can designate the foreign currency borrowing as a fair value hedge of foreign currency risk attributable to its foreign equity investment. In those circumstances, the foreign equity investment is retranslated at each balance sheet date and exchange difference arising on the retranslation is recognised in profit or loss to offset the exchange difference arising on the retranslation of the foreign currency borrowings. However, the hedging criteria set out in paragraph 88 of IAS 39 must still be met in order to achieve fair value hedge accounting in the reporting entity's separate financial statements. Whether, in practice, such a parent entity would apply hedge accounting in its separate financial statements may well depend on the tax treatment of undertaking such hedging activities.

Foreign operations in hyper-inflationary economies

7.109 Where a foreign entity operates in a country in which a very high rate of inflation exists and its functional currency is the local currency, the closing rate/net investment method is not suitable for translating the foreign entity's financial statements for inclusion in the consolidated financial statements. This is because an asset acquired in a currency that is the currency of a hyper-inflationary economy may be worth very little at a time of high inflation, when the foreign currency has

© 2013 PricewaterhouseCoopers LLP. All rights reserved.

类为其他综合收益。

7.108.2　IAS 27 指出，合并财务报表中包括的对子公司、共同控制主体和联营企业的投资在母公司的单独财务报表中以成本计量、或者按 IAS 39 进行核算。这意味着权益投资既可以按成本减去减值计量，可以被指定为“可供出售”或者被指定为“公允价值变动计入损益”（如果 IAS 39 允许的话）。IAS 27 要求对于投资的各个类别使用相同的会计处理。问题在于，在境外权益投资按成本计价的情况下，在主体的单独财务报表中，外币借款是否可以被指定为该主体的境外权益投资的套期。IAS 39 对于净投资套期的规定只适用于合并财务报表。然而，我们认为报告主体可以指定外币借款为可归属于其境外权益投资的外币风险的公允价值套期。在该等情况下，境外权益投资在各资产负债表日被重新折算，由重新折算产生的汇兑差额被记录在损益中，以抵销外币借款重新折算产生的汇兑差额。然而，为了在单独财务报表中达到公允价值套期会计处理，报告主体必须依然符合 IAS 39 第 88 段所列出的套期标准。实务操作中，该母公司主体是否应该会在单独财务报表中采用套期会计处理，很可能取决于对从事此类套期活动的税务处理。

恶性通货膨胀经济中的境外经营

7.109　当境外主体在一个存在极高通货膨胀率的国家中经营且其功能货币是当地货币的情况下，按期末汇率/净投资法来折算该境外主体财务报表以包括在合并财务报表中是不合适的。这是因为，当外币对报告主体功能货币已极度贬值时，以该恶性通货膨胀经济中的货币所购入的资产在高度通货膨胀时期可能所值无几，由此导致一个大额借项被计入合并权益中的准备。同时，包括在合并利润表中该境外主体的经营成果被夸大了（无论来自迅速贬值的

© 2013 普华永道（PricewaterhouseCoopers）版权所有。

weakened considerably against the reporting entity's functional currency, leading to a large debit to consolidated reserves. At the same time, the results of the foreign entity are included at an inflated amount in the consolidated income statement (whether from high interest income on deposits in a rapidly depreciating foreign currency or from trading operations that could be considered to reflect unrealistically high profitability). Therefore, as money loses purchasing power in a hyper-inflationary economy, the reporting of operating results and financial position in the local currency without adjustment to reflect current price levels is misleading.

7.110 When an entity's functional currency is the currency of the hyper-inflationary economy, the entity applies IAS 29. For information on the accounting treatment for entities operating in hyper-inflationary economies, refer to chapter 31.

[The next paragraph is 7.115.]

Presentation and disclosure

General

7.115 The paragraphs that follow deal with IAS 21's disclosure requirements that apply to both individual financial statements and consolidated financial statements. IFRS 7 requires significant additional disclosures about foreign currency transactions and activities. The requirements of IFRS 7 are dealt with in chapter 11 of IFRS Manual of Accounting – Financial Instruments.

Accounting policies

7.116 There is no specific requirement in IAS 21 to disclose accounting policies in respect of foreign currency transactions. This is because IAS 1 requires disclosure of significant policies that are relevant to an entity's financial statements. [IAS 1 para 108]. In respect of foreign currency transactions, the accounting

© 2013 PricewaterhouseCoopers LLP. All rights reserved.

外币存款所产生的超高利息收入，还是来自可能被认为超乎实际能力的高盈利购销业务)。所以，当货币在恶性通货膨胀经济中失去购买力时，如果不做调整以反映出现实的价格水平，以当地货币报告的经营成果和财务状况是误导性的。

7.110　当主体的功能货币为恶性通货膨胀经济的货币时，主体适用于 IAS 29。有关恶性通货膨胀经济中经营主体的会计处理，参考第三十一章。

[下一段为第 7.115 段。]

列报和披露

一般原则

7.115　以下段落讨论同时适用于个别财务报表和合并财务报表在 IAS 21 中的披露要求。IFRS 7 要求对关于外币交易和业务活动进行重大的额外披露。这些 IFRS 7 的要求在《国际财务报告准则实务指引——金融工具系列》第十一章中进行阐述。

会计政策

7.116　IAS 21 没有对如何披露关于外币交易的会计政策提出具体要求。这是因为 IAS 1 要求了披露与主体财务报表相关的重大政策。[IAS 1 第 108 段]。关于外币交易的会计政策附注至少应当说明用于外币交易及境外经营（包含那些在恶性通货膨胀经济中的境外经营）财务报表的折算方法以及对于汇兑

ⓒ 2013 普华永道（PricewaterhouseCoopers）版权所有。

policy note should state, as a minimum, the methods used in translating foreign currency transactions and the financial statements of foreign operations including those operating in hyper-inflationary economies, and the treatment accorded to exchange differences. The following is an example of a foreign currency accounting policy.

Table 7. 1 – Accounting policy for foreign currency

Heineken N. V. – Report and accounts – 31 December 2011

2. Basis of preparation (extract)

(c) Functional and presentation currency

These consolidated financial statements are presented in euro, which is the Company's functional currency. All financial information presented in euro has been rounded to the nearest million unless stated otherwise.

3. Significant accounting policies (extract)

(b) Foreign currency

(i) Foreign currency transactions

Transactions in foreign currencies are translated to the respective functional currencies of HEINEKEN entities at the exchange rates at the dates of the transactions. Monetary assets and liabilities denominated in foreign currencies at the reporting date are retranslated to the functional currency at the exchange rate at that date. The foreign currency gain or loss arising on monetary items is the difference between amortised cost in the functional currency at the beginning of the period, adjusted for effective interest and payments during the period, and the amortised cost in foreign currency translated at the exchange rate at the end of the reporting period.

Non-monetary assets and liabilities denominated in foreign currencies that are measured at fair value are retranslated to the functional currency at the exchange rate at the date that the fair value was determined.

Non-monetary items in a foreign currency that are measured in terms of historical cost are translated using the exchange rate at the date of the transaction. Foreign currency differences arising on retranslation are recognised in profit or loss, except for differences arising on the retranslation of available-for-sale (equity) investments and foreign currency

© 2013 PricewaterhouseCoopers LLP. All rights reserved.

差额的处理方法。下面为外币会计政策的一个示例。

图表 7.1——对于外币的会计政策

Heineken N. V. ——报告与报表——2011 年 12 月 31 日

2. 编制基础（摘要）

（c）功能和列报货币

这些合并财务报表以本公司的功能货币欧元进行列报。除非另有说明，所有以欧元列报的财务信息已被四舍五入至“百万元”。

3. 重大会计政策（摘要）

（b）外币

（i）外币交易

以外币计价的交易按交易日的汇率被折算为 HEINEKEN 各个主体各自的功能货币。以外币计价的货币性资产和负债以报告日的汇率被重新折算为功能货币。从货币性项目中所产生的外币利得或损失为功能货币于期初的摊余成本（经报告期期间实际利息和付款的调整后）与按报告期期末汇率折算的外币摊余成本之间的差额。

以公允价值计量的以外币计价的非货币性资产和负债，按公允价值确定日的汇率被重新折算为功能货币。

以历史成本计量的外币非货币性项目按交易日的汇率进行折算。除了产生于可供出售（权益）投资的重新折算和产生于被指定为净投资套期的金融负债的重新折算被确认为其他综合收益以外，重新折算产生的外币差额被确认为损益。

ⓒ 2013 普华永道（PricewaterhouseCoopers）版权所有。

Con.

differences arising on the retranslation of a financial liability designated as a hedge of a net investment, which are recognised in other comprehensive income.

Non-monetary assets and liabilities denominated in foreign currencies that are measured at cost remain translated into the functional currency at historical exchange rates.

(ii) Foreign operations

The assets and liabilities of foreign operations, including goodwill and fair value adjustments arising on acquisition, are translated to euro at exchange rates at the reporting date. The income and expenses of foreign operations, excluding foreign operations in hyperinflationary economies, are translated to euro at exchange rates approximating the exchange rates ruling at the dates of the transactions. Group entities, with a functional currency being the currency of a hyperinflationary economy, first restate their financial statements in accordance with IAS 29, Financial Reporting in Hyperinflationary Economies (see 'Reporting in hyperinflationary economies' below). The related income, costs and balance sheet amounts are translated at the foreign exchange rate ruling at the balance sheet date.

Foreign currency differences are recognised in other comprehensive income and are presented within equity in the translation reserve. However, if the operation is a non-wholly-owned subsidiary, then the relevant proportionate share of the translation difference is allocated to the non-controlling interests. When a foreign operation is disposed of such that control, significant influence or joint control is lost, the cumulative amount in the translation reserve related to that foreign operation is reclassified to profit or loss as part of the gain or loss on disposal. When HEINEKEN disposes of only part of its interest in a subsidiary that includes a foreign operation while retaining control, the relevant proportion of the cumulative amount is reattributed to non-controlling interests. When HEINEKEN disposes of only part of its investment in an associate or joint venture that includes a foreign operation while retaining significant influence or joint control, the relevant proportion of the cumulative amount is reclassified to profit or loss.

Foreign exchange gains and losses arising from a monetary item receivable from or payable to a foreign operation, the settlement of which is neither planned nor likely in the foreseeable future, are considered to form part of a net investment in a foreign operation and are recognised in other comprehensive income, and are presented within equity in the translation reserve.

The following exchange rates, for the most important countries in which HEINEKEN has operations, were used while preparing these consolidated financial statements:

© 2013 PricewaterhouseCoopers LLP. All rights reserved.

续表

以成本计量的外币非货币性资产和负债仍按历史汇率折算为功能货币。

（ii）境外经营

境外经营的资产和负债（包含收购产生的商誉和公允价值调整）按报告日汇率折算为欧元。境外经营的收入和费用（除了在恶性通货膨胀经济中的境外经营）按近似于交易日的汇率被折算为欧元。当恶性通货膨胀经济中的货币为其功能货币，集团中的各主体首先根据 IAS 29 在恶性通货膨胀经济中进行财务报告（参见下文中的“在恶性通货膨胀经济中进行报告”）重述其财务报表。相关的收入、成本和资产负债表金额按资产负债表日的汇率被折算为欧元。

确认在其他综合收益中的外币差额被列报为权益中的折算准备。然而，如果该经营为非全资子公司，则相应比例份额的折算差额被分配至非控制性权益。当处置一个境外经营使得主体丧失对其控制权、重大影响或共同控制权时，折算准备中与该境外经营相关的累计金额作为处置利得或损失的一部分被重分类至损益。当 HEINEKEN 在保留控制权的同时，仅处置其在子公司（包含一个境外经营）中的部分权益时，相应比例的累计金额被重新归属于非控制性权益。当 HEINEKEN 在保留重大影响或共同控制权的同时，仅处置其在联营或合营投资（包含一个境外经营）中的部分权益时，相应比例的累计金额被重分类至损益。

对境外经营的一项应收或应付货币性项目，在可预见的将来既未打算也不大可能结算，被作为对该境外经营净投资的组成部分，由其产生的汇兑利得和损失在其他综合收益中予以确认，并列报为权益中的折算准备。

以下汇率是 HEINEKEN 在其有经营的数个最重要国家里用于编制这些合并财务报表时所使用的汇率：

ⓒ 2013 普华永道（PricewaterhouseCoopers）版权所有。

Con.

	Year-end		Average	
In EUR	2011	2010	2011	2010
BRL	**0.4139**	0.4509	**0.4298**	0.4289
GBP	**1.1972**	1.1618	**1.1522**	1.1657
MXN	**0.0554**	0.0604	**0.0578**	0.0598
NGN	**0.0049**	0.0050	**0.0047**	0.0051
PLN	**0.2243**	0.2516	**0.2427**	0.2503
RUB	**0.0239**	0.0245	**0.0245**	0.0248
USD	**0.7729**	0.7484	**0.7184**	0.7543

(iii) Reporting in hyperinflationary economies

When the economy of a country in which we operate is deemed hyperinflationary and the functional currency of a Group entity is the currency of that hyperinflationary economy, the financial statements of such Group entities are adjusted so that they are stated in terms of the measuring unit current at the end of the reporting period. This involves restatement of income and expenses to reflect changes in the general price index from the start of the reporting period and, restatement of non-monetary items in the balance sheet, such as P, P & E to reflect current purchasing power as at the period end using a general price index from the date when they were first recognised. Comparative amounts are not adjusted. Any differences arising were recorded in equity on adoption.

(iv) Hedge of net investments in foreign operations

Foreign currency differences arising on the retranslation of a financial liability designated as a hedge of a net investment in a foreign operation are recognised in other comprehensive income to the extent that the hedge is effective and regardless of whether the net investment is held directly or through an intermediate parent. These differences are presented within equity in the translation reserve. To the extent that the hedge is ineffective, such differences are recognised in profit or loss. When the hedged part of a net investment is disposed of, the relevant amount in the translation reserve is transferred to profit or loss as part of the profit or loss on disposal.

© 2013 PricewaterhouseCoopers LLP. All rights reserved.

续表

兑欧元	年末 2011	年末 2010	平均 2011	平均 2010
巴西雷亚尔	**0.4139**	0.4509	**0.4298**	0.4289
英镑	**1.1972**	1.1618	**1.1522**	1.1657
墨西哥比索	**0.0554**	0.0604	**0.0578**	0.0598
尼日利亚奈拉	**0.0049**	0.0050	**0.0047**	0.0051
波兰兹罗提	**0.2243**	0.2516	**0.2427**	0.2503
俄罗斯卢布	**0.0239**	0.0245	**0.0245**	0.0248
美元	**0.7729**	0.7484	**0.7184**	0.7543

(iii) 在恶性通货膨胀经济中进行报告

当我们在一个被视为恶性通货膨胀经济中的国家里经营且集团中的那一个主体的功能货币是该恶性通货膨胀经济中的货币时，此类集团中的主体的财务报表应进行调整以使其按照报告期末日的计量单位进行表述。这涉及对收益和费用的重述以反映自报告期期初起一般物价指数的变化以及对资产负债表中的非货币性项目（例如不动产、工厂和设备）的重述，以反映他们自初始确认日起使用一般物价指数计算的期末现时购买力。比较金额无需进行调整。产生的任何差额应在采用该准则时记录于权益中。

(iv) 对境外经营净投资的套期

重新折算被指定为境外经营净投资套期的金融负债所产生的外币差额，以套期的有效部分为限，在其他综合收益中进行确认，而不管该净投资被直接还是通过中间层面母公司来持有。这些差额列报为权益中的折算准备。在无效套期的范围内，这些差额在损益中予以确认。当处置净投资的套期部分时，折算准备中的相关金额应作为处置利得或损失的一部分被转至损益。

ⓒ 2013 普华永道（PricewaterhouseCoopers）版权所有。

Disclosure

7.117 In respect of exchange differences, IAS 21 requires disclosure of:

- The amount of exchange differences recognised in profit or loss except for those arising on financial instruments measured at 'fair value through profit or loss' in accordance with IAS 39.

- Net exchange differences recognised in other comprehensive income and classified in a separate component of equity and a reconciliation of the amount of such exchange differences at the beginning and end of the period.

[IAS 21 para 52].

7.118 The disclosure required above is on an aggregate net basis. The total amount of exchange differences recognised in profit or loss include exchange differences recognised on subsequent settlement and retranslation to closing rate on balances arising on foreign currency transactions. However, the standard is silent as to where in profit or loss they should be included. A cue can be taken from IAS 12, which states that exchange differences arising on foreign deferred tax assets and liabilities may be included as part of the deferred tax expense (income) if that presentation is considered to be the most useful to financial statement users. Therefore:

- Foreign exchange differences arising from trading transactions may be included in the results of operating activities.

- Foreign exchange differences arising from financing may be included as a component of finance cost/income.

7.118.1 The following examples illustrate the disclosure of the recognition of exchange differences in profit or loss and as a separate component in equity.

© 2013 PricewaterhouseCoopers LLP. All rights reserved.

披露

7.117　关于汇兑差额，IAS 21 要求披露：

- 除那些依据 IAS 39 计量的“以公允价值计量且其变动计入当期损益”的金融工具所产生的汇兑差额以外，在损益中所确认的汇兑差额的金额。

- 在其他综合收益中所确认的被分类为单列权益项目的净汇兑差额以及此类汇兑差额期初金额和期末金额的调节。

[IAS 21 第 52 段]。

7.118　以上所要求的披露是以合计净额为基础的。损益中所确认的汇兑差额总额包括后续结算以及对外币交易产生的余额按期末汇率重新折算所确认的汇兑差额。然而，准则并未提及汇兑差额应当被包含在损益中的哪个地方。从以下 IAS 12 的描述中能够得到一个提示，如果该列报被认为对于财务报表使用者最为有用的话，产生于境外递延所得税资产和负债的汇兑差额可能被包含在递延所得税费用（收益）中，作为其组成部分。因此：

- 购销交易产生的汇兑差额可能被包含在经营活动成果中。

- 融资产生的汇兑差额可能被包含在融资成本/收益中作为其组成部分。

7.118.1　以下的几个示例就披露损益中所确认的汇兑差额以及作为单列权益项目所确认的汇兑差额进行了说明。

ⓒ 2013 普华永道（PricewaterhouseCoopers）版权所有。

Table 7.2 – Disclosure of exchange differences recognised in profit or loss

Associated British Foods plc – Report and accounts – 17 September 2011

2. Operating costs (extract)

	Note	2011 £m	2010 £m
OPERATING COSTS ARE STATED AFTER CHARGING/(CREDITING):			
Employee benefits expense	3	**1,613**	1,497
Amortisation of non-operating intangibles	8	**83**	81
Amortisation of operating intangibles	8	**13**	8
Profits less losses on disposal of non-current assets		**(5)**	9
Depreciation of owned property, plant & equipment	9	**317**	324
Operating lease payments under property leases		**110**	95
Operating lease payments for hire of plant & equipment		**13**	11
Other operating income		**(19)**	(14)
Research and development expenditure		**24**	22
Fair value gains on financial assets and liabilities held for trading		**(29)**	(27)
Fair value losses on financial assets and liabilities held for trading		**24**	31
Foreign exchange gains on operating activities		**(35)**	(40)
Foreign exchange losses on operating activities		**38**	38

4. Interest and other finance income and expense

	2011 £m	2010 £m
FINANCE INCOME		
Interest income on financial assets not at fair value through profit or loss		
– cash and cash equivalents	**9**	11
– finance leases	–	1
Total finance income	**9**	12
FINANCE EXPENSE		
Interest expense on financial liabilities not at fair value through profit or loss:		
– bank loans and overdrafts	**(48)**	(34)
– all other borrowings	**(45)**	(46)
– finance leases	**(1)**	(1)
– other payables	**(3)**	(3)
– unwinding of discount on provisions	**(4)**	(4)
Total finance expense	**(101)**	(88)

© 2013 PricewaterhouseCoopers LLP. All rights reserved.

图表 7.2——披露损益中所确认的汇兑差额

Associated British Foods plc——报告和报表——2011 年 9 月 17 日

2. 营业成本(摘要)

	附注	**2011 年 百万英镑**	**2010 年 百万英镑**
所列营业成本——记入/(贷记)之后:			
职工福利费用	3	**1,613**	1,497
非经营性无形资产的摊销	8	**83**	81
经营性无形资产的摊销	8	**13**	8
非流动资产的处置利得减去损失		**(5)**	9
所拥有的不动产、工厂和设备的折旧	9	**317**	324
不动产租赁下的经营租赁付款		**110**	95
租用工厂和设备的经营租赁付款		**13**	11
其他营业收益		**(19)**	(14)
研究和开发支出		**24**	22
交易性金融资产和负债的公允价值利得		**(29)**	(27)
交易性金融资产和负债的公允价值损失		**24**	31
经营活动的汇兑利得		**(35)**	(40)
经营活动的汇兑损失		**38**	38

4. 利息和其他财务收入和费用

	2011 年 百万英镑	**2010 年 百万英镑**
财务收入		
非以公允价值计量且其变动计入当期损益的金融资产的利息收入		
— 现金和现金等价物	**9**	11
— 融资租赁	–	1
财务收入合计	**9**	12
财务费用		
非以公允价值计量且其变动计入当期损益的金融负债的利息费用:		
— 银行借款和透支	**(48)**	(34)
— 所有其他借款	**(45)**	(46)
— 融资租赁	**(1)**	(1)
— 其他应付款	**(3)**	(3)
— 转回被折现后的准备	**(4)**	(4)
财务费用合计	**(101)**	(88)

ⓒ 2013 普华永道（PricewaterhouseCoopers）版权所有。

Con.

OTHER FINANCIAL INCOME			
Expected return on employee benefit scheme assets	12	**149**	188
Interest charge on employee benefit scheme liabilities	12	(**142**)	(143)
Net financial income in respect of employee benefit schemes		**7**	(5)
Net foreign exchange gains/(losses) on financing activities		–	(3)
Total other financial income		**7**	(8)

Table 7.3 – Disclosure of exchange differences recognised in a separate component of equity

Xstrata plc – Report and accounts – 31 December 2011

26. Capital and Reserves (extract)

Other reserves

US $ m	Revaluation reserves	Other reserves	Net unrealised gains (losses)	Foreign currency translation	Total
At 31 December 2009	1,440	1,229	188	2,749	5,606
Gains on available-for-sale financial assets	–	–	118	–	118
Realised losses on available-for-sale financial assets	–	–	(73)	–	(73)
Gains on cash flow hedges	–	–	117	–	117
Realised losses on cash flow hedges *	–	–	(131)		(131)
Foreign currency translation differences	–	–	–	2,459	2,459
Deferred tax	–	–	(9)	(48)	(57)
At 31 December 2010	1,440	1,229	210	5,160	8,039
Gains on available-for-sale financial assets	–	–	37)	–	37)
Realised gains on available-for-sale financial assets	–	–	(8)	–	(8)
Gains on cash flow hedges	–	–	26	–	26
Realised gains on cash flow hedges *	–	–	(51)	–	(51)
Foreign currency translation differences	–	–	–	(1,309)	(1,309)
Deferred tax	–	–	19	2	21
At 31 December 2011	**1,440**	**1,229**	**159**	**3,853**	**6,681**

* Recycled gains of US $ 59 million (2010 US $ 115 million) are included in Revenue in the income statement, including non-controlling interests.

© 2013 PricewaterhouseCoopers LLP. All rights reserved.

续表

其他财务收入			
职工福利计划资产的预期回报	12	**149**	188
职工福利计划负债的利息费用	12	**(142)**	(143)
与职工福利计划有关的净财务收入		**7**	(5)
筹资活动的净汇兑利得/(损失)		–	(3)
其他财务收入合计		**7**	(8)

图表 7.3——披露单列权益项目中所确认的汇兑差额

Xstrata plc——报告和报表——2011 年 12 月 31 日

26. 资本和准备(摘要)

其他准备

	重估价准备	其他准备	未实现净利得(损失)	外币折算	合计
百万美元					
于 2009 年 12 月 31 日	1,440	1,229	188	2,749	5,606
可供出售金融资产的利得	–	–	118	–	118
可供出售金融资产的已实现损失	–	–	(73)	–	(73)
现金流量套期的利得	–	–	117	–	117
现金流量套期的已实现损失*	–	–	(131)		(131)
外币折算差额	–	–	–	2,459	2,459
递延所得税	–	–	(9)	(48)	(57)
于 2010 年 12 月 31 日	1,440	1,229	210	5,160	8,039
可供出售金融资产的利得	–	–	37)	–	37)
可供出售金融资产的已实现利得	–	–	(8)	–	(8)
现金流量套期的利得	–	–	26	–	26
现金流量套期的已实现利得*	–	–	(51)	–	(51)
外币折算差额	–	–	–	(1,309)	(1,309)
递延所得税	–	–	19	2	21
于 2011 年 12 月 31 日	**1,440**	**1,229**	**159**	**3,853**	**6,681**

* 利润表的收入及非控制性权益中包含被转出的利得 5,900 万美元（2010 年：1.15 亿美元）。

ⓒ 2013 普华永道（PricewaterhouseCoopers）版权所有。

Con.

Revaluation reserves

This reserve principally records the remeasurement from cost of the 19.9% interest held in Falconbridge Limited (Falconbridge) to the fair value of 19.9% of the identifiable net assets of Falconbridge on 15 August 2006, the date the Group obtained control of Falconbridge.

Other reserves

This reserve principally originated during 2002 from the merger of Xstrata AG into Xstrata plc of US $ 279 million and the issue of shares from the acquisition of the Duiker and Enex Groups of US $ 935 million.

Net unrealised gains/(losses) reserve

This reserve records the remeasurement of available-for-sale financial assets to fair value (refer to note 22) and the effective portion of the gain or loss on cash flow hedging contracts (refer to notes 23, 29 and 36). Deferred tax is provided on the remeasurement at tax rates enacted or substantively enacted.

Foreign currency translation reserve

This is used to record exchange differences arising from the translation of the financial statements of foreign subsidiaries. It is also used to record the exchange differences from the translation of quasi equity inter-company loans in foreign operations. On disposal or partial disposal of a foreign entity, the deferred accumulated amount recognised in this reserve is transferred to the income statement.

7.119 The standard permits a reporting entity to present its financial statements in a currency that is different from its functional currency. In this situation, the following should be disclosed:

- The fact that the presentation currency is different from the functional currency.
- The disclosure of the functional currency.
- The reasons for using a different presentation currency.

[IAS 21 para 53].

In these cases the entity provides the foreign currency risk disclosures required by

© 2013 PricewaterhouseCoopers LLP. All rights reserved.

续表

重估价准备 这一准备主要记录了集团在取得控制权之日（2006 年 8 月 15 日）按照 Falconbridge 有限公司（Falconbridge）19.9% 的可辨认净资产的公允价值对所持 Falconbridge 19.9% 的权益投资成本进行的重新计量。 **其他准备** 这一准备主要由 2002 年度期间 Xstrata AG 与 Xstrata plc 合并而产生的 2.79 亿美元以及为收购 Duiker and Enex 集团发行股票而产生的 9.35 亿美元。 **未实现净利得/(损失)准备** 这一准备记录了对可供出售金融资产(参考附注 22）按公允价值的重新计量以及现金流量套期合同有效部分的利得或损失(参考附注 23、29 和 36)。在重新计量时根据已颁布或实质上已完成立法的税率确认了递延所得税。 **外币折算准备** 这是用来记录折算境外子公司财务报表所产生的汇兑差额。也用于记录折算境外经营的公司间准权益贷款所产生的汇兑差额。在处置或部分处置境外主体时，确认在该准备中的递延累计金额被转至利润表。

7.119　该准则允许报告主体以一种不同于其功能货币的货币列报其财务报表。在这种情况下，应当披露以下信息：

- 列报货币不同于功能货币这一事实情况。
- 功能货币的披露。
- 使用一种不同列报货币的理由。

[IAS 21 第 53 段]。

在这些示例中，主体按照 IFRS 7 的要求提供关于其功能货币而非列报货币的

© 2013 普华永道（PricewaterhouseCoopers）版权所有。

IFRS 7 in reference to its functional currency rather than its presentation currency. The entity's exposure to currencies other than the functional currency will affect its future performance, and the details of these exposures are provided in the financial statements.

Table 7.4 – Presentation currency differs from functional currency

DP World Limited – Report and accounts – 31 December 2011

2. Basis of preparation (extract)

(d) Functional and presentation currency

The functional currency of the Company is UAE Dirhams. Each entity in the Group determines its own functional currency and items included in the financial statements of each entity are measured using that functional currency.

These consolidated financial statements are presented in United States Dollars ("USD"), which in the opinion of management is the most appropriate presentation currency in view of the global presence of the Group. All financial information presented in USD is rounded to the nearest thousand.

UAE Dirham is currently pegged to USD and there are no differences on translation from functional to presentation currency.

7.120 When there is a change in the functional currency of either the reporting entity or a significant foreign operation, that fact and the reason for the change in functional currency is disclosed. [IAS 21 para 54]. As changes in functional currency may be due to a number of reasons, it is not possible to say what disclosure might be required in a particular case. However, it will certainly require a more substantial disclosure than, for example, 'this currency was chosen because it gives the most appropriate presentation'. Table 7.5 below is an example where the entity's functional currency is changed, but the presentation currency has remained the same as the latter was already in dollars. Table 7.5.1 is a situation where both the functional currency of the parent (see para 7.46) and the parent and group's presentation currency (see para 7.82) are changed. The parent accounts under UK GAAP, but the relevant standard, FRS 23, is the same as IAS 21 in all material respects.

© 2013 PricewaterhouseCoopers LLP. All rights reserved.

外币风险披露。主体对非功能货币的风险敞口将影响其未来业绩，此类风险敞口的详细情况应在财务报表中予以提供。

图表 7.4——列报货币不同于功能货币

DP World Limited ——报告和报表——2011 年 12 月 31 日

2. 编制基础（摘要）

（d）功能和列报货币

本公司的功能货币是阿联酋迪拉姆。集团中的各主体决定各自的功能货币，并使用该功能货币对包含在各主体财务报表中的项目进行计量。

这些合并财务报表以美元（“USD”）列报，管理层认为鉴于集团的全球性地位，美元是最合适的列报货币。所有以美元列报的财务信息均四舍五入至“千元”。

阿联酋迪拉姆目前与美元挂钩，由功能货币折算成列报货币没有折算差额。

7.120 当无论报告主体、还是重大境外经营变更功能货币时，应披露变更功能货币这一事实情况和理由。[IAS 21 第 54 段]。由于变更功能货币可能是由于多种原因造成的，所以不可能对某一特定的情况所应作出的披露作出规定。然而，要求作出的披露肯定要比后面的例子更具有实质性，例如：“选择该货币是因为它能给予最适当的列报”。下面的图表 7.5 是一个在主体变更其功能货币，但保持列报货币不变，因后者已经是美元情况下的示例。图表 7.5.1 是一个在母公司的功能货币（参见第 7.46 段）、母公司及集团的列报货币（参见第 7.82 段）两者均被变更情况下的情形。母公司报表根据英国一般公认会计原则进行编制，其相关准则（英国财务报告准则第 23 号）在所有重大方面与 IAS 21 相同。

ⓒ 2013 普华永道（PricewaterhouseCoopers）版权所有。

Table 7. 5 – Change of functional currency

Royal Dutch Shell plc – Report and accounts – 31 December 2005

3. Accounting policies (extract)

Change in functional currency

Following Royal Dutch Shell becoming the parent company of Royal Dutch and Shell Transport on July 20, 2005 and through Royal Dutch and Shell Transport, of the rest of the Shell Group, the Directors have concluded that the most appropriate functional currency of the Company is dollars. This reflects the fact that the majority of the Shell Group's business is influenced by pricing in international commodity markets, with a dollar economic environment. The previous functional currency of the Company was the euro.

On the date of the change of functional currency all assets, liabilities, issued capital and other components of equity and income statement items were translated into dollars at the exchange rate on that date. As a result the cumulative currency translation differences which had arisen up to the date of the change of functional currency were reallocated to other components within equity (refer to Note 13).

As a result of the change in functional currency the Company's functional and presentation currency are now the same.

13. Other reserves (extract)

Cumulative currency translation differences

Cumulative currency translation differences represent the currency differences which arose as a result of translating the financial statements from the Company's previous functional currency of euro to the reporting currency of dollars.

The impact of the change in functional currency was the reallocation at that date of the cumulative currency translation differences of $15 million to issued capital.

Table 7. 5. 1 – Change of functional and presentation currencies

Smith & Nephew plc – Annual report – 31 December 2006

NOTES TO THE PARENT COMPANY ACCOUNTS (extract)

A. General Information (extract)

Presentation of Financial Information

The Company redenominated its share capital into US Dollars on 23 January 2006 and will

© 2013 PricewaterhouseCoopers LLP. All rights reserved.

图表 7.5——功能货币的变更

Royal Dutch Shell plc——报告和报表——2005 年 12 月 31 日

3. 会计政策（摘要）

功能货币的变更

随着 Royal Dutch Shell 于 2005 年 7 月 20 日成为 Royal Dutch 和 Shell Transport 的母公司并通过 Royal Dutch 和 Shell Transport 成为 Shell Group 其余各公司的母公司，董事会已作出结论，最适合本公司的功能货币是美元。这反映了 Shell Group 多数业务受到美元经济环境下国际商品市场定价的影响这一事实情况。本公司的原功能货币是欧元。

于功能货币变更日，所有资产、负债、已发行股本、权益的各其他组成部分以及利润表项目均按照当日汇率被折算为美元。因此，截至功能货币变更之日已经产生的累计货币折算差额在权益的各其他组成部分之间被重新分配（参考附注 13）。

功能货币的变更导致本公司的功能货币与列报货币现在是相同的。

13. 其他准备（摘要）

累计货币折算差额

累计货币折算差额是指将本公司的财务报表由原功能货币欧元折算为列报货币美元所产生的货币差额。

变更功能货币的影响为累计货币折算差额 150 万美元于变更日被重新分配至已发行股本。

图表 7.5.1——功能和列报货币的变更

Smith & Nephew plc——年度报告——2006 年 12 月 31 日

母公司报表附注（摘要）

A. 一般信息（摘要）

财务信息列报

本公司于 2006 年 1 月 23 日以美元对其股本重新计价，并以美元来保留可分配准备金

ⓒ 2013 普华永道（PricewaterhouseCoopers）版权所有。

Con.

retain distributable reserves and declare dividends in US Dollars. Consequently its functional currency became the US Dollar. Financial information for prior periods has been restated from Sterling into US Dollars in accordance with FRS 23. As a result the presentational currency of the Company (i. e. US Dollars) in the restated 2005 accounts is different from the functional currency of the Company.

Share capital and share premium in comparative periods was translated at the rate of exchange on the date of redenomination.

NOTES TO THE GROUP ACCOUNTS (extract)

Presentation of financial information

As the Group's principal assets and operations are in the US and the majority of its operations are conducted in US Dollars, the Group changed its presentational currency from Pounds Sterling to US Dollars with effect from 1 January 2006. The Company redenominated its share capital into US Dollars on 23 January 2006 and will retain distributable reserves and declare dividends in US Dollars. Consequently its functional currency became the US Dollar. This lowers the Group's exposure to currency translation risk on its revenue, profits and equity. Financial information for prior periods has been restated from Pounds Sterling into US Dollars in accordance with IAS 21.

The cumulative translation reserve was set to nil at 1 January 2003 (i. e. the transition date to IFRS). All subsequent movements comprising differences on the retranslation of the opening net assets of non US Dollar subsidiaries and hedging instruments have been charged to the cumulative translation reserve included in 'Other Reserves'. Share capital and share premium was translated at the rate of exchange on the date of redenomination.

As a result of the above the presentational currency of the Group (i. e. US Dollars) in the restated years of 2005 and 2004 is different from the functional currency of the Company (i. e. Pounds sterling).

In previous years the Group protected its equity, as measured in Sterling, by matching non-Sterling assets with non-Sterling liabilities principally by the use of currency swaps. Exchange movements on both the non-Sterling net assets and the hedging instruments were recorded as movements in 'Other Reserves'. As hedging was effective up to the date of the change in functional currency, the Group has continued to present these as movements in 'Other Reserves' as this hedging is regarded as valid in the comparator years. When presenting comparative periods in US Dollars the retranslation of the net Sterling assets results in the large exchange differences shown in the Statement of Recognised Income and Expense.

© 2013 PricewaterhouseCoopers LLP. All rights reserved.

续表

和宣告股利。因而，导致其功能货币变更为美元。按照英国财务报告准则第 23 号，已将前期财务信息由英镑变更为美元并进行了重述。因此，本公司经重述后 2005 年度报表的列报货币（也就是美元）不同于本公司的功能货币。

多个可比期间的股本和股本溢价按照重新计价之日的汇率进行了折算。

集团报表附注（摘要）

财务信息列报

由于本集团的主要资产和业务在美国并以美元开展多数业务，本集团将列报货币由英镑变更为美元，自 2006 年 1 月 1 日起生效。本公司于 2006 年 1 月 23 日以美元对其股本重新计价，并以美元来保留可分配准备金和宣告股利。因而，导致其功能货币变更为美元。此举降低了本集团的收入、利润及权益的货币折算风险敞口。依据 IAS 21，已将多个以前期间的财务信息由英镑变更为美元并进行了重述。

累计折算准备于 2003 年 1 月 1 日（也就是国际财务报告准则转换日）被归零。所有的后续变动（包括非美元子公司期初净资产和套期工具的重新折算差额）已被计入累计折算准备并包含在“其他准备”中。股本和股本溢价按重新采用计价货币之日的汇率进行了折算。

上述原因导致本集团于 2005 年和 2004 年的重述年度的列报货币（即美元）不同于本公司的功能货币（即英镑）。

在以前的年度中，本集团对非英镑资产和非英镑负债进行匹配并主要通过使用货币互换来保护其以英镑计量的权益。非英镑净资产和套期工具的汇兑变动均作为“其他准备”的变动进行记录。直至功能货币变更日之前，由于各比较年度所进行的套期是有效的，本集团已继续将其作为“其他准备”的变动进行列报。当以美元列报多个比较期间时，对英镑净资产的重新折算导致大额汇兑差额被列示于已确认利得和损失表中。

ⓒ 2013 普华永道（PricewaterhouseCoopers）版权所有。

Table 7.5.2 – Change of functional and presentation currencies

Sibir Energy plc – Annual report – 31 December 2007

NOTES TO THE COMPANY FINANCIAL STATEMENTS (extract)

1. SIGNIFICANT ACCOUNTING POLICIES (extract)

Foreign currencies

Presentational currency

Given that the functional currency of the Company is now US Dollars, management have elected to present for the first time Company financial statements in US Dollars.

This is a change from prior years when the financial statements were presented in pound sterling in line with the previous functional currency of the Company.

Change in presentational currency

For the 2006 comparative period, assets and liabilities were translated into US Dollars using the closing rate ruling at the 2006 balance sheet date ($/£1.9572).

Equity and Share capital items were translated using the historic closing rate applicable on 1 January 2005 and were not re translated at each subsequent balance sheet date. All share capital transactions which were effected after 1 January 2005 were recorded using an exchange rate which prevailed at the date of those transactions.

Resulting exchange differences were reflected as currency translation adjustments and included in the cumulative currency translation reserve.

The applicable exchange rates used for 2005 and 2006 were:

	US Dollar to Pound Sterling Exchange Rate ($/£)		
Date	01/01/2005	31/12/2005	31/12/2006
Av Rate	–	1.8188	1.8369
Closing Rate	1.9212	1.7167	1.9572

NOTES TO THE CONSOLIDATED FINANCIAL STATEMENTS (extract)

2. SUMMARY OF SIGNIFICANT ACCOUNTING POLICIES (extract)

Presentational currency

In the 2006 financial statements, the functional currency of Sibir Energy plc (the Company) was Pound Sterling. Although the Company is domiciled in the UK the Group's operations are based in the Russian Federation. The functional currency of the Group's various entities is either the Russian Rouble or US Dollar. This is due to the direct or

© 2013 PricewaterhouseCoopers LLP. All rights reserved.

图表 7.5.2——功能和列报货币的变更

Sibir Energy plc——年度报告——2007 年 12 月 31 日

公司财务报表附注(摘要)

1. 重大会计政策(摘要)

外币

列报货币

鉴于本公司现在的功能货币是美元，管理层已选择首次以美元列报其公司财务报表。

这是相对于以前数年度的一个变更，当时的财务报表以英镑进行列报，与本公司的原功能货币保持一致。

列报货币的变更

对于 2006 年度比较期间，资产和负债按 2006 年度资产负债表日的期末汇率（美元/英镑 1.9572）被折算为美元。

权益和股本项目按适用于 2005 年 1 月 1 日的历史期末汇率进行折算且不在其后各资产负债表日进行重新折算。所有在 2005 年 1 月 1 日之后生效的股本交易，以那些交易日的现时汇率进行记录。

所造成的汇兑差额反映为货币折算调整并被包含在累计货币折算准备中。

2005 年和 2006 年使用的适用汇率为：

	美元对英镑的汇率（美元/英镑）		
日期	2005 年 1 月 1 日	2005 年 12 月 31 日	2006 年 12 月 31 日
平均汇率	–	1.8188	1.8369
期末汇率	1.9212	1.7167	1.9572

合并财务报表附注（摘要）

2. 重大会计政策汇总（摘要）

列报货币

在 2006 年度财务报表中，Sibir Energy plc（本公司）的功能货币是英镑。虽然本公司的所在地为英国，但本集团业务基地在俄罗斯联邦。集团各主体的功能货币或为俄罗斯卢布，或为美元。这是因为石油和石油产品的价格是与美元发生直接的或间接的链接，即便是在有些交易以卢布来定价和结算的时候。因此，与 2007 年度财务报表一

ⓒ 2013 普华永道（PricewaterhouseCoopers）版权所有。

Con.

indirect linkage of oil and oil product prices to the US Dollar, even when some trades are priced and settled in Roubles. As a result the 2006 financial comparatives together with the 2007 financial statements have been presented in US Dollars ($).

This is a change from prior years and the Group's last published interims when the financial statements were presented in Pound Sterling.

Assets and liabilities were translated into US Dollars using the closing rate at the 2006 balance sheet date. Income, expenses and cash flows recognised in the period were translated at an average US Dollar exchange rate for the period. Resulting exchange differences were reflected as currency translation adjustments and included in the cumulative currency translation reserve.

Equity and share capital items were translated using the historic closing rate applicable on 1 January 2005 and were not re translated at each subsequent balance sheet date. All share capital transactions which were effected after 1 January 2005 were recorded using an exchange rate which prevailed at the date of those transactions.

The applicable exchange rates used for 2006 were:

Period Ended	1 January 2006	31 December 2006
Average	0.5498	0.5444
Closing Rate	0.5825	0.5109

7.121 When an entity presents its financial statements in a currency that is different from its functional currency, it describes the financial statements as complying with International Financial Reporting Standards only if they comply with all the requirements of each applicable standard and each applicable interpretation of those standards including the translation method set out in paragraphs 7.77 and 7.109 above.

Convenience translation

7.122 IAS 21 does not prohibit an entity from providing, as supplementary information, a 'convenience translation'. Such a convenience translation may display financial statements or other financial information (such as five year summaries) in a currency that is not its functional currency or its presentation

© 2013 PricewaterhouseCoopers LLP. All rights reserved.

续表

同列报的2006年度财务比较数据已经以美元（$）进行了列报。

这是相对于以前数年度和本集团最近发表的中期报告的一个变更，当时的财务报表是以英镑进行列报的。

资产和负债按2006年度资产负债表日的期末汇率被折算为美元。报告期内所确认的收益、费用及现金流量以该报告期的平均美元汇率进行折算。所造成的汇兑差额反映为货币折算调整并被包含在累计货币折算准备中。

权益和股本项目按适用于2005年1月1日的历史期末汇率进行折算且不在其后各资产负债表日进行重新折算。所有在2005年1月1日之后生效的股本交易，以那些交易日的现时汇率进行记录。

2006年使用的适用汇率为：

止期间	2006年1月1日	2006年12月31日
平均汇率	0.5498	0.5444
期末汇率	0.5825	0.5109

7.121 当主体以不同于其功能货币的货币列报其财务报表时，只有在财务报表遵循每一个适用的准则以及适用于那些准则的每一项解释（包括上述第7.77段和第7.109段所规定的折算方法）的所有规定时，主体才可称其财务报表遵循国际财务报告准则。

简易折算

7.122 IAS 21不禁止主体提供“简易折算”作为补充信息。这种简易折算可能既不以其功能货币、也不以其列报货币的货币列示财务报表或其他财务信息（诸如五年汇总），以方便于某些使用者。简易折算一般对出现在以功能货币或列报货币列报的财务报表中的所有金额适用单一汇率进行编制。财务报

ⓒ 2013 普华永道（PricewaterhouseCoopers）版权所有。

currency, as convenience to some users. Convenience translations are normally prepared by applying a single exchange rate to all amounts appearing in financial statements presented in the entity's functional or presentation currency. The relationships among amounts in the financial statements do not change. Thus, convenience translation fails to account for the effects of changes in foreign exchange rates and, therefore, does not comply with the translation procedures set out in paragraphs 7.77 above. Therefore, where an entity displays its financial statements or other financial information in a currency that is different from either its functional currency or its presentation currency and the requirements of paragraph 7.121 above are not met, it should:

■ Clearly identify the information as supplementary information to distinguish it from the information that complies with International Financial Reporting Standards.

■ Disclose the currency in which the supplementary information is displayed.

■ Disclose the entity's functional currency and the method of translation used to determine the supplementary information.

[IAS 21 para 57].

Table 7.6 – Disclosure for convenience translation

OJSC RBC – Report and accounts – 31 December 2010

2. Basis of preparation (extract)

(c) Functional and presentation currency

The national currency of the Russian Federation is the Russian Rouble ("RUR") which is the Group's functional currency and the currency in which these consolidated financial statements are presented. All financial information presented in RUR has been rounded to the nearest million.

(d) Convenience translation

In addition to presenting the consolidated financial statements in RUR, supplementary information in the US Dollars ("USD") has been presented for the convenience of users of the financial statements.

All amounts in the consolidated financial statements, including comparatives, are translated from RUR to USD at the closing exchange rate at 31 December 2010 of RUR 30.4769 to USD 1.

© 2013 PricewaterhouseCoopers LLP. All rights reserved.

表中各金额之间的关系保持不变。所以，简易折算无法核算汇率变动所造成的影响，因而未遵循上述第 7.77 段所规定的折算程序。所以在主体以既不同于其功能货币、也不同于其列报货币的货币列示其财务报表或其他财务信息且不符合上述第 7.121 段所要求的情况下，主体应当：

- 清晰地将该信息识别为补充信息，以将其与遵循国际财务报告准则的信息区分开来。
- 披露用于列示补充信息的货币。
- 披露主体的功能货币以及用于确定补充信息的折算方法。

[IAS 21 第 57 段]。

图表 7.6——对简易折算的披露

OJSC RBC——报告和报表——2010 年 12 月 31 日

2. 编制基础（摘要）

(c) 功能和列报货币

俄罗斯联邦的国家货币俄罗斯卢布（“RUR”）是本集团的功能货币以及这些合并财务报表的列报货币。所有以 RUR 列报的财务信息已被四舍五入至“百万元”。

(d) 简易折算

在以 RUR 对合并财务报表进行列示之外，为方便财务报表使用者，以美元（“USD”）列示了补充信息。

合并报表中的所有金额（包括比较数据）按照 2010 年 12 月 31 日的汇率（30.4769 卢布兑 1 美元）由卢布折算为美元。

© 2013 普华永道（PricewaterhouseCoopers）版权所有。

Other matters

Tax effects of all exchange differences

7.123 Gains and losses on foreign currency transactions and exchange differences arising on the translating the results and financial position of an entity (including a foreign operation) into a different currency may have tax effects. IAS 12 applies to these tax effects, and the issues are considered in chapter 13.

Cash flow statements

7.124 Cash flows arising from transactions in foreign currency and cash flows of a foreign subsidiary are translated at the exchange rates between the functional currency and the foreign currency at the dates of the cash flows. IAS 7 applies to foreign currency cash flows, which is addressed in chapter 30.

© 2013 PricewaterhouseCoopers LLP. All rights reserved.

其他事项

所有汇兑差额的所得税影响

7.123　外币交易利得和损失以及将主体（包括一个境外经营）的经营成果和财务状况折算为不同货币所产生的汇兑差额可能影响其所得税。这些所得税影响适用 IAS 12，此类问题在第十三章中进行阐述。

现金流量表

7.124　外币交易所引起的现金流量以及境外子公司的现金流量按照现金流量发生日的汇率在功能货币和外币之间进行折算。外币现金流量适用 IAS 7，在第三十章中进行阐述。

ⓒ 2013 普华永道（PricewaterhouseCoopers）版权所有。

PwC Assurance Service Contacts
联系普华永道审计业务部

北京 Beijing
梁伟坚 Thomas Leung
电话 Tel：+86（10）6533 2838
电子邮件 Email：thomas. w. leung@ cn. pwc. com

上海 Shanghai
李丹 Daniel Li
电话 Tel：+86（21）2323 3388
电子邮件 Email：daniel. li@ cn. pwc. com

重庆 Chongqing
李松波 Bobby Lee
电话 Tel：+86（23）6393 7388
电子邮件 Email：bobby. lee@ cn. pwc. com

深圳 Shenzhen
张展豪 Albert Cheung
电话 Tel：+86（755）8261 8833
电子邮件 Email：albert. cheung@ cn. pwc. com

大连 Dalian
关兆文 Dorman Kwan
电话 Tel：+86（411）8379 1666
电子邮件 Email：dorman. kwan@ cn. pwc. com

苏州 Suzhou
汪超 Arthur Wang
电话 Tel：+86（512）6273 1998
电子邮件 Email：arthur. wang@ cn. pwc. com

广州 Guangzhou
何国辉 Timothy Ho
电话 Tel：+86（20）3819 2888
电子邮件 Email：timothy. kf. ho@ hk. pwc. com

天津 Tianjin
郑广安 Kwong On Cheng
电话 Tel：+86（22）2318 3003
电子邮件 Email：kwong. on. cheng@ cn. pwc. com

青岛 Qingdao
张国俊 Kevin Zhang
电话 Tel：+86（532）8089 1818
电子邮件 Email：kevin. zhang@ cn. pwc. com

西安 Xi'an
叶骏 Joe Ye
电话 Tel：+86（29）8720 3998
电子邮件 Email：joe. ye@ cn. pwc. com

PwC Accounting Consulting Services Contacts
联系普华永道会计专业咨询服务

金以文 Yvonne Kam
电话 Tel：+86（21）2323 3267
电子邮件 Email：yvonne. kam@ cn. pwc. com

陈保郎 Baolang Chen
电话 Tel：+86（21）2323 2555
电子邮件 Email：baolang. chen@ cn. pwc. com

方毅贤 Ian Farrar
电话 Tel：+852 2289 2313
电子邮件 Email：ian. p. farrar@ hk. pwc. com

陈燕华 Tracy Chen
电话 Tel：+86（21）2323 3070
电子邮件 Email：tracy. yh. chen@ cn. pwc. com

许心莹 Samying Huie
电话 Tel：+86（10）6533 2965
电子邮件 Email：samying. s. huie@ cn. pwc. com

苏虹 Shelley So
电话 Tel：+852 2289 2955
电子邮件 Email：shelley. so@ hk. pwc. com

© 2013 PricewaterhouseCoopers LLP. All rights reserved.

沈洁 Jie Shen
电话 Tel：+86（21）2323 3659
电子邮件 Email：jie. shen@ cn. pwc. com

白鸿安 Hendry Pai
电话 Tel：+86（10）6533 7760
电子邮件 Email：hendry. pai@ cn. pwc. com

陈嘉怡 Clarry Chan
电话 Tel：+852 2289 2169
电子邮件 Email：clarry. chan@ hk. pwc. com

吴慧莹 Monica Ng
电话 Tel：+852 2289 1218
电子邮件 Email：monica. wy. ng@ hk. pwc. com

阮慧瑶 Elza Yuen
电话 Tel：+852 2289 2314
电子邮件 Email：elza. yuen@ hk. pwc. com

梁少宝 Dorothy Leung
电话 Tel：+852 2289 2151
电子邮件 Email：dorothy. sp. leung@ hk. pwc. com

戴奈尔 Nigel Dealy
电话 Tel：+852 2289 1221
电子邮件 Email：nigel. dd. dealy@ hk. pwc. com

孙宇辉 Yuhui Sun
电话 Tel：+86（10）6533 7331
电子邮件 Email：yuhui. sun@ cn. pwc. com

For further help, please contact:
如需更多帮助，请联系：

北京 Beijing
中国北京市
朝阳区东三环中路7号
北京财富中心写字楼A座26楼
邮政编码 100020
26/F Office Tower A
Beijing Fortune Plaza
7 Dongsanhuan Zhong Road
Chaoyang District
Beijing 100020, PRC
电话 Tel：+86（10）6533 8888
传真 Fax：+86（10）6533 8800

大连 Dalian
中国大连市西岗区中山路147号
森茂大厦8楼
邮政编码 116011
8/F Senmao Building
147 Zhongshan Road
Xigang District
Dalian 116011, PRC
电话 Tel：+86（411）8379 1888
传真 Fax：+86（411）8379 1800

重庆 Chongqing
中国重庆市渝中区邹容路68号
大都会商厦19楼1905室
邮政编码 400010
Room 1905
19/F Metropolitan Tower
68 Zou Rong Road
Chongqing 400010, PRC
电话 Tel：+86（23）6393 7888
传真 Fax：+86（23）6393 7200

广州 Guangzhou
中国广州市天河区珠江新城
珠江西路10号
普华永道中心18楼
邮政编码 510623
18/F PwC Center
10 Zhujiang Xi Road
Pearl River New City
Tianhe District
Guangzhou 510623, PRC
电话 Tel：+86（20）3819 2000
传真 Fax：+86（20）3819 2100

ⓒ 2013 普华永道（PricewaterhouseCoopers）版权所有。

杭州 Hangzhou
中国杭州市下城区环城北路 208 号
坤和中心 3205 室
邮政编码 310006
Room 3205, Canhigh Center
208 Huancheng Road North
Xiacheng District
Hangzhou 310006, PRC
电话：+86（571）2807 6388
传真：+86（571）2807 6300

宁波 Ningbo
中国宁波市江东区民安东路 268 号
宁波国际金融服务中心 E 座 1203 室
邮政编码 315040
Room 1203, Tower E
Ningbo International Financial Center
268 Min An Road East
Jiangdong District
Ningbo 315040, PRC
电话 Tel：+86（574）8187 1788
传真 Fax：+86（574）8187 1700

香港 Hong Kong
中国香港中环太子大厦 22 楼
22/F Prince's Building
Central
Hong Kong, PRC
电话 Tel：+852 2289 8888
传真 Fax：+852 2810 9888

青岛 Qingdao
中国青岛市市南区延安三路 234 号
海航万邦中心 1 号楼 37 楼
邮政编码 266071
37/F Tower One, HNA IMC Center
234 Yanan Third Road, Shinan District
Qingdao 266071, PRC
电话 Tel：+86（532）8089 1888
传真 Fax：+86（532）8089 1800

澳门 Macau
中国澳门苏亚利斯博士大马路 323 号
中国银行大厦 29 楼
29/F Bank of China Building
323 Avenida Doutor Mario Soares
Macau, PRC
电话 Tel：+853 8799 5111
传真 Fax：+853 8799 5222

上海 Shanghai
中国上海市黄浦区湖滨路 202 号
企业天地 2 号楼
普华永道中心 11 楼
邮政编码 200021
11/F PwC Center
2 Corporate Avenue
202 Hu Bin Road
Huangpu District
Shanghai 200021, PRC
电话 Tel：+86（21）2323 8888
传真 Fax：+86（21）2323 8800

南京 Nanjing
中国南京市鼓楼区中央路 201 号
南京国际广场南塔 12A 层 01 室
邮政编码 210009
Room 12A01, South Tower
Nanjing International Center
201 Zhongyang Road
Gulou District
Nanjing 210009, PRC
电话 Tel：+86（25）6608 6288
传真 Fax：+86（25）6608 6210

深圳 Shenzhen
中国深圳市罗湖区深南东路 5016 号
京基 100 － A 座 34 楼
邮政编码 518001
34/F Tower A, Kingkey 100
5016 Shennan East Road
Luohu District
Shenzhen 518001, PRC
电话 Tel：+86（755）8261 8888
传真 Fax：+86（755）8261 8800

© 2013 PricewaterhouseCoopers LLP. All rights reserved.

新加坡 Singapore
新加坡 048424 邮区
PWC 大厦
克罗士街 8 号 17 楼
8 Cross Street # 17 – 00
PWC Building
Singapore 048424
电话 Tel：+65 6236 3388
传真 Fax：+65 6236 3300

天津 Tianjin
中国天津市和平区
南京路 189 号
津汇广场 2 座 36 楼
邮政编码 300051
36/F The Exchange Tower Two
189 Nanjing Road
Heping District
Tianjin 300051，PRC
电话 Tel：+86（22）2318 3333
传真 Fax：+86（22）2318 3300

苏州 Suzhou
中国苏州市苏州工业园区
旺墩路 188 号建屋大厦 1501 室
邮政编码 215028
Room 1501，Genway Tower
188 Wang Dun Road
Suzhou Industrial Park
Suzhou 215028，PRC
电话 Tel：+86（512）6273 1888
传真 Fax：+86（512）6273 1800

厦门 Xiamen
中国厦门市思明区鹭江道 8 号
国际银行大厦 11 楼 B 室
邮政编码 361001
Unit B，11/F
International Plaza
8 Lujiang Road
Siming District
Xiamen 361001，PRC
电话 Tel：+86（592）210 7888
传真 Fax：+86（592）210 8800

台湾 Taiwan
中国台北市信义区 110
基隆路一段 333 号 27 楼
International Trade Building
27F，333 Keelung Road，Section 1
Taipei 110，Taiwan
电话 Tel：+886 2 2729 6666
传真 Fax：+886 2 2757 6371

西安 Xi'an
中国西安市南关正街 88 号
长安国际中心 D 座 7 楼
邮政编码 710068
7/F，D Block，Chang'an Metropolis Center
88 Nanguan Street
Xi'an 710068，PRC
电话 Tel：+86（29）8469 2688
传真 Fax：+86（29）8469 2600

如欲了解更多资讯，敬请登陆公司网站：
For more information，please visit our websites at：
pwccn. com
pwchk. com

ⓒ 2013 普华永道（PricewaterhouseCoopers）版权所有。

图书在版编目（CIP）数据

国际财务报告准则实务指引．第7章，外币：汉英对照/陈保郎等编译．—北京：中国财政经济出版社，2013.5

（普华永道国际财务报告准则实务指引系列）

ISBN 978-7-5095-4433-4

Ⅰ.①国… Ⅱ.①陈… Ⅲ.①会计准则-世界-汉、英 Ⅳ.①F233.1

中国版本图书馆CIP数据核字（2013）第076704号

责任编辑：吴 敏　　　　责任校对：黄亚青

中国财政经济出版社出版

URL：http：//www.cfeph.cn

E-mail：cfeph@cfeph.cn

（版权所有 翻印必究）

社址：北京市海淀区阜成路甲28号 邮政编码：100142

营销中心电话：88190406 北京财经书店电话：64033436 84041336

北京富生印刷厂印刷 各地新华书店经销

787×1092毫米 16开 14印张 240 000字

2013年11月第1版 2013年11月北京第1次印刷

定价：36.00元

ISBN 978-7-5095-4433-4/F·3591

（图书出现印装问题，本社负责调换）

本社质量投诉电话：010-88190744

反盗版举报热线：88190492、88190446